FLORIDA CIVIL WAR BLOCKADES

BLOCKADES

Battling for the Coast

NICK WYNNE &
JOE CRANKSHAW

Charleston   London

THE
History
PRESS

Published by The History Press
Charleston, SC 29403
www.historypress.net

Copyright © 2011 by Nick Wynne and Joe Crankshaw
All rights reserved

First published 2011

Manufactured in the United States

ISBN 978.1.60949.340.0

Library of Congress Cataloging-in-Publication Data

Wynne, Nick.
Florida Civil War blockades : battling for the coast / Nick Wynne and Joe Crankshaw.
p. cm.
ISBN 978-1-60949-340-0
1. Florida--History--Civil War, 1861-1865--Blockades. 2. United States--History--Civil
War, 1861-1865--Blockades. 3. Florida--History--Civil War, 1861-1865--Naval operations.
4. United States--History--Civil War, 1861-1865--Naval operations. I. Crankshaw, Joe. II.
Title.
E600.W96 2011
973.7'459--dc23
2011025153

For Debra T. Wynne and Cynthia Putnam Crankshaw

Contents

Introduction

Every kingdom divided against itself is brought to desolation; and every city or house divided against itself shall not stand.
—Matthew 12:25

The great conflict that ravaged the United States during the first five years of the 1860s was the product of years of political, economic and moral wrangling between citizens of the Southern states and their brethren in the Northern ones. In 1832, the Nullification Crisis, which saw South Carolinians seek to declare a protective tariff null and void within the boundaries of their state, raised the specter of secession and of state rights taking precedence over federal laws. President Andrew Jackson made preparations to invade South Carolina, and citizens of that state began their own preparations to defend South Carolina. Only the passage of a compromise tariff defused the situation. In 1850, the question of secession was raised again when Congress attempted to limit the expansion of slavery into new territories acquired by the United States. Once again, radical politicians in South Carolina called for the breakup of the Union and the creation of a separate Southern nation that would protect slavery and preserve the agrarian values that had dominated the early federal government and American society. The secession of the Southern states was avoided when moderate and conservative leaders persuaded radicals that compromise was possible, particularly since Southerners controlled most of the important committees of Congress. The Compromise of 1850, among other things, protected the institution of slavery in new territories below 36° 30' and outlawed the slave trade in the District of Columbia, but the compromise merely delayed future conflicts because it did not address the fundamental issues of state secession and the institution of slavery.

During the decade of the 1850s, the rise of the abolitionist movement and the Republican Party exacerbated sectional differences. As the voices on both sides of the slavery debate became more strident and political leaders more radicalized, the chances for a lasting compromise grew smaller and smaller. The growing industrialization of Northern states, fueled by growing hordes of European immigrants, saw the South losing its economic importance and its influence in the political life of the nation.

Men like Robert Toombs, Alexander Stephens and Howell Cobb of Georgia, who had led the moderates in Nashville in 1850, slowly moved to more radical positions, frustrated by the election of ideologues to public office in Northern states, Southern states and Congress. Sadly, they concluded that the Union, which had seen so many Southerners as leading lights, was in its death throes. The election of Abraham Lincoln, a moderate abolitionist, in 1860 was the final straw, and these moderates, and others like them throughout the South, became reluctant secessionists. Only an independent Southern nation, in their opinion, could preserve Southern institutions like slavery and state rights. If the Southern states remained in the Union, they would be reduced to a secondary role, subject to the will of the more populous Northern states. It was better, they reasoned, to disband the Union and create a smaller, heterogeneous nation of slave owners and small farmers bound together by an agrarian economy.

With Lincoln's election, Southern radicals gained the upper hand, and on December 20, 1861, South Carolina left the Union. South Carolina's action was quickly duplicated by six additional slave states—Alabama, Florida, Georgia, Louisiana, Mississippi and Texas—and on February 8, 1861, the establishment of the Confederate States of America was announced at a convention of delegates from these now independent nations in Montgomery, Alabama. Governors of the various Confederate states hurriedly sent state militia troops to occupy Federal property and military establishments within their state borders. Two major installations—Fort Pickens in Pensacola and Fort Sumter in Charleston Harbor—remained in Federal hands when the commanders of these forts refused to surrender them to state troops. Federal control of Fort Taylor in Key West was not challenged, since it was so far from other occupied parts of Florida that it could not be taken. Key West would play a major role in the Union's later war plans.

INTRODUCTION

With Lincoln's inauguration in March 1861, Americans—North and South—wondered what his stance would be toward the Confederacy and the takeover of Federal property. In April, he made the decision to resupply Fort Sumter. This event triggered a Confederate bombardment of Sumter on April 12, which forced the fort to surrender. The war that both sides did not wish was now a reality.

As a result of the outbreak of violence at Fort Sumter, four additional Southern states—Virginia, North Carolina, Tennessee and Arkansas—cast their lot with the Confederacy, and each side prepared for war. Union and Confederate leaders were sure that any war would be one of a short duration, and each side felt that it had advantages to ensure a win. Southern leaders pointed to the fact that their military heritage (many of the high-ranking prewar officers in the United States Army were Southerners) and the martial traditions of Southern state militias would give it an advantage, while Union leaders felt that they possessed a winning hand because the Union retained control of the navy and the major stores of military equipment. Abraham Lincoln was so certain that the war would be concluded in a matter of weeks or months that his initial call for volunteers asked for only 75,000 men to "suppress the rebellion." The Provisional Confederate Congress, meeting in Montgomery, authorized newly elected Confederate president Jefferson Davis to call for 100,000 volunteers. Both sides miscalculated, and the war went on for four long years.

The Confederate government was pledged to the defense of the new Southern nation, and the notion of defense dominated its strategy for war. Given the limited military resources of the different Confederate states and the central government, a defensive strategy made sense. The major consideration for Confederate leaders was simply to hold the territory they had, not to expand or to add new territory. Only when the opportunity to deal a devastating blow to Union armies arose would the Confederate forces abandon the defense and move to the offense. Tragically for Confederate military fortunes, Robert E. Lee took the Army of Northern Virginia into Union territory twice, and both invasions ended miserably for the Confederacy.

On the ocean, however, Confederate cruisers and privateers carried out an aggressive campaign against Union naval vessels and commercial ships. Unfettered by the need to defend fixed positions or to occupy territory, Confederate ships were free to roam the oceans preying on isolated victims. Because the Confederate navy was small and composed of a variety of warships—most purchased abroad or converted from existing merchant ships—it was impractical to conduct fleet exercises or to assemble a large fleet to confront the more numerous Union navy in a single battle. By necessity, the Confederate naval ships operated as lone wolves, dangerous and ready to strike at every opportunity.

The persistence of small, shallow-draft vessels—blockade runners—ferrying supplies to Southern ports and coasts aided the offensive capabilities of the small Confederate navy because stopping these activities tied up hundreds of Union ships. The need for task-specific ships to implement the Federal blockade and to support army activities on the various rivers that split the Confederacy required the expenditure of millions of dollars and delayed the construction of larger cruisers by the United States. Both nations relied on captured or purchased ships to supplement their naval forces, a situation that favored the Union because of its larger resources.

For Union leaders, defense of Federal territory was a secondary consideration because restoration of the pre-1860 United States required the conquest of Southern states that had seceded. Thus, the concept of fighting an offensive war on land and at sea dominated Federal military thinking. The emphasis on offensive warfare placed greater demands on the Union and required the development of larger land and naval forces.

Florida Civil War Blockades: Battling for the Coast looks at one aspect of the Union's naval war efforts—the blockade of the 1,500 miles of Florida coasts to stop the importation of civilian and military supplies from European and Caribbean nations and to eliminate the export of Southern agricultural products as a source of money and diplomatic power.

Chapter 1

In the Beginning

We rely greatly on the sure operation of a complete blockade of the Atlantic and Gulf ports soon to commence. In connection with such blockade we propose a powerful movement down the Mississippi to the ocean, with a cordon of posts at proper points, and the capture of Forts Jackson and Saint Philip; the object being to clear out and keep open this great line of communication in connection with the strict blockade of the seaboard, so as to envelop the insurgent States and bring them to terms with less bloodshed than by any other plan.
—Winfield Scott, May 3, 1861

With these words, written in a letter to Major General George B. McClellan, Lieutenant General Winfield Scott, the commanding general of the United States Army, proposed a key part of the Federal strategy for winning the Civil War. Although Scott, who had served as an American general for forty-seven years, would soon retire from active service and although his plan for enveloping and splitting the Confederacy would soon be modified by other generals, his basic proposal to isolate the Confederate states and to split the Confederacy remained largely intact. Labeled the Anaconda Plan by Unionist newspapers, Scott's proposal was based on the idea that quick and decisive action by Federal land and naval forces would bring a rapid end to the rebellion. It was not to be, however, and the War Between the States lasted for four long years at the cost of almost two million casualties of all kinds.

Above: Aged Winfield Scott, the top United States general in 1861, proposed his Anaconda Plan—as it was labeled in the press—to split the Confederacy and blockade its ports. *Courtesy of the Wynne Collection.*

Left: Winfield Scott was an American hero from the Mexican-American War. When the Civil War started, Scott decided he was too old and infirm to lead the Union army. *Courtesy of the Wynne Collection.*

In the Beginning

The essence of Scott's plan was to implement a naval blockade of the three thousand miles of Confederate coastline from Virginia to Texas and prevent the importation of critical war supplies and to ensure that the Confederate government could not wield economic pressure on European nations—dependent on Southern cotton—to gain diplomatic recognition or military assistance. The plan was flawed from the beginning because the Union navy consisted of only a few ships, most of which were designed for open ocean sailing, not shallow coastal waters. Although the Federal government embarked on a crash program of building a "ninety-day" navy through the purchase of existing merchant ships and the construction of small coastal warships, progress was slow. Additionally, manning such ships required recruiting crews from merchant vessels and training raw recruits for sea duty. As a result, the blockade, when first adopted, was porous and easily circumvented by ships of the Confederate navy, as well as by privately owned Southern blockade runners. Even at war's end in 1865, blockade runners and Confederate ships of war continued to be effective. For example, the CSS *Shenandoah*, under the command of James Iredell Waddell, continued to operate against Union commercial interests until late June 1865, two months after Robert E. Lee's surrender at Appomattox Court House and Abraham Lincoln's assassination. There were persistent rumors, although none can be substantiated, that Africans continued to be imported for use as slaves at the height of the Civil War.

Confederate military and political leaders were no slouches, and they quickly directed state militias to take control of the series of coastal forts—Fort Clinch, Fort Pulaski and Fort Pickens—that provided protection for blockade runners at Fernandina, Savannah and Pensacola. Although Fort Clinch and Fort Pulaski were quickly brought under Southern control, Fort Pickens was occupied by Federal troops and remained in Union hands throughout the war. Some forts, like Fort Taylor in Key West and Fort Jefferson in the Dry Tortugas, remained under the control of Union forces. Key West was simply too far down Florida's landmass and difficult to access for Confederate forces to occupy and hold. So, too, was Fort Jefferson, which was even more difficult to capture and hold successfully. Both of these forts became important cogs in the blockade for Union ships. Lesser fortifications, like those at Apalachicola, passed in and out of Union and Confederate hands throughout the war. Robert E. Lee, who had been a secretary of a panel that conducted a survey of these forts prior to the outbreak of hostilities, recommended to Confederate president Jefferson Davis that these forts be held, if possible, but with little expenditure of men and equipment, and abandoned if Southern possession was directly challenged by a Federal invasion.

Above: Fort Taylor became the stronghold of the Union army in Key West. The Federal army and navy quickly took control of the coastal forts on the Florida peninsula. *Courtesy of the Ada E. Parrish Postcard Collection.*

Left: Robert E. Lee was offered command of the Union army by General Winfield Scott, but he refused to take sides against his native state of Virginia. He served the Confederacy initially by conducting an engineering survey of coastal fortifications in 1861. *Courtesy of the Wynne Collection.*

In the Beginning

Florida, the third Southern state to secede, had few resources to dedicate to protecting coastal fortifications on its own. With barely 145,000 residents—half of whom were slaves—the Sunshine State was sparsely populated, and most of the 15,000 Floridians who served in the Confederate forces were sent to fight as part of Lee's Army of Northern Virginia or in the western theater of the war—Tennessee, Mississippi or Louisiana—under Braxton E. Bragg and Joseph E. Johnston. Quickly, Federal forces, already in possession of Key West and Pensacola, secured control of Fort Marion (Castillo de San Marcos) in St. Augustine, the port at Cedar Key with its railroad connection and the critically vital deepwater port at Jacksonville, which was occupied four times by the Union army. The early capture of Fort Clinch effectively blocked the direct shipment of war materiel and civilian supplies into Fernandina. The closing of these ports also prevented the out-shipment of beef, pork and salt to Rebel armies in more northern Confederate ports.

Unlike more developed Southern states, when war came in 1861, Florida had only one cross-state railroad, which had opened in 1860 and ran from Fernandina to Cedar Key. With the Union control of both ends of the road, it was quickly abandoned as a major transportation artery, and the rails from that road were ripped up and used to build shorter lines connecting Florida with larger, longer railroads in Georgia and Alabama. Cedar Key became

Fort Marion in St. Augustine, formerly known as the Castillo de San Marcos, quickly fell to Florida state troops in 1861, although it was eventually abandoned to Union forces in 1861. *Courtesy of the Florida State Photographic Archives.*

The city of St. Augustine was occupied by Federal troops through most of the war. It became a haven for runaway slaves and Florida Unionists. *Courtesy of the Florida State Photographic Archives.*

a staging point for Union ships and minor incursions of Federal troops into the interior of the state. Seahorse Key, which effectively controlled entrance and exit from the harbor at Cedar Key, became a refugee camp for Floridians loyal to the Union cause and a prisoner of war camp for captured Confederates. Even after it was occupied by the Union forces, Cedar Key played only a minor role in the war.

Still, Florida's 1,500 miles of coastline presented a vexing problem to Federal military leaders, who envisioned hundreds of small blockade runners landing and unloading critically needed war materiel in the thousands of small inlets and bays along the coast. On the Atlantic side of the Sunshine State, the Indian River Lagoon, 155 miles long and protected against Union warships by barrier islands, presented a particularly onerous task to the Union navy to control. Mosquito Inlet, near present-day New Smyrna Beach, also offered numerous opportunities from small sloops and flat-bottomed steamships to land cargo unobserved since its shallow waters effectively blocked entrance by large seagoing vessels of the Union navy.

Added to the mission of the blockading ships was the job of finding, preventing and destroying thousands of small salt manufacturing operations, usually consisting of little more than a few copper kettles, fueled by driftwood and manned by a few men. The long coast and

In the Beginning

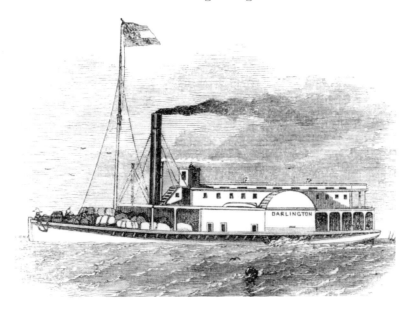

The *Darlington*, which was captured by Union naval vessels in Fernandina, was typical of the small steamers used by blockade runners to evade the larger ships of the Union navy. Its shallow draft allowed it to avoid the main channels of a harbor and escape capture by using small creeks and inlets. *Courtesy of the Wynne Collection.*

Saltworks were scattered along the coasts of Florida and produced tons of this much-needed preservative. Destroying saltworks became part of the routine duties of sailors on the vessels of the East Gulf Blockading Squadron. Harper's Weekly, *1862. Courtesy of the Florida State Photographic Archives.*

hundreds of broad beaches presented countless opportunities for Confederates to construct such distilleries overnight with little difficulty. Salt was such a valuable commodity—used in food preparation and the manufacture of gunpowder—that interior states sent special units to Florida's coasts for the purpose of distilling seawater and harvesting the salt residue. After the Confederacy instituted a draft, salt workers were exempted from military service.

Florida's long coastline also presented myriad opportunities for small sailing vessels and steamers to head out of Florida ports, loaded with cotton, cattle and tobacco, for Southern destinations. Cuba, the Bahamas and the ports of Mexico and Central America were popular places to carry the agricultural products of Florida, Alabama, Louisiana, Mississippi and Texas. Once off-loaded, Southern exports could be sold and the money used to purchase military and civilian supplies, which were ferried back to the Confederacy. Once again, the Union navy faced the difficult challenge of stopping these operations, a task that it never completed successfully throughout the war.

Like the United States, the Confederate States had a navy, and like the Union, the Confederacy, which had no ships at all when the war began, purchased existing tonnage from commercial enterprises in Southern states or European companies or commissioned entirely new ships to be built at French and British shipyards. As the need for more ships grew, including ironclad riverine vessels, Confederate shipyards were constructed in several small cities. As the war dragged on, Confederate naval strategists began to envision a fleet of ironclads, heavily armored and steam powered, that could slip from small coastal harbors to wreak havoc with ships of the Union blockade and to offer protection for blockade runners.

Finally, the Union navy had to deal with the problems of establishing a supply line for its blockading ships, constructing new naval bases or modifying and expanding old ones; creating a waterborne medical system for dealing with diseases and wounds and housing; and feeding captured Confederate seamen. Training sufficient numbers of sailors to man the vessels of the blockade was a time-consuming but necessary task, because few of the merchant seamen of the day had experience in gunnery or were familiar with the rules of military service. Since one of the major tools used to recruit able-bodied seamen for Union ships was the opportunity to participate in the prize money from captured ships and cargoes, a workable system of naval courts to deal with confiscated ships and cargo had to be established. Existing federal and state courts in those areas under Union control had little experience with the international protocols that regulated the process.

In the Beginning

The Federal navy consisted of a mere seventy-six vessels of all types when the blockade was ordered on April 19, 1861, and of these ships, only forty-two were in adequate repair to be used. Of the forty-two, thirty Federal ships were on station in foreign waters, which left twelve for use as blockaders. Of these twelve, only four ships, which carried a complement of 280 men and twenty-five guns, were pressed into immediate service.

Lincoln might easily proclaim a blockade of the Southern coasts, but it would exist primarily on paper for most of 1861 and early 1862. The lack of available ships meant that only a few harbors could be patrolled, but even then, Confederate shore batteries prevented the establishment of an effective blockade. Some ships that might have been added to the blockade fleet were ordered to work in support of Union army movements and to sail up navigable rivers as far as possible to destroy Confederate gun emplacements. In addition, some Union ships were periodically utilized to carry individuals from Confederate territories who, under a flag of truce, desired to join families or friends in Northern states. These demands further reduced the ability of the Federal navy to carry out its assigned responsibilities.

For the first several months, the Union navy proved to be ineffective in carrying out Lincoln's order to blockade Southern ports and failed to stop movement into and out of these ports by Confederate or foreign ships. Gideon Welles, the Union secretary of the navy, reminded Flag Officer S.H. Stringham, the first commander of the Federal blockading force, that "a lawful maritime blockade requires the actual presence of an adequate force stationed at the entrance of the port sufficiently near to prevent communication." Welles also reminded Stringham that "the only exception to this rule which requires the actual presence of an adequate force to constitute a lawful blockade arises out of the circumstance of the occasional temporary absence of the blockading squadron, produced by accident, as in the case of a storm, which does not suspend the legal operation of a blockade. The law considers an attempt to take advantage of such an accidental removal a fraudulent attempt to break the blockade."

The small number of available Union ships negated widespread enforcement of the blockade and raised the specter of possible war with France and England over it. According to the Declaration of Paris, an 1856 treaty that defined the rights of neutrals and the requirements for a blockade, any recognized blockade had to be effective to be legal, and such was not the case for the United States. Although the United States was not a signatory to this international pact, Lincoln and Welles tried mightily to establish some semblance of effectiveness as a means of preventing European recognition of the Confederacy, but this was difficult to do convincingly.

The Confederate government recognized the need for diplomatic recognition very soon after the creation of the Confederate States. In February 1861, Robert Toombs, the Southern secretary of state, sent a three-man delegation to Europe to convince hesitant leaders there that recognition was deserved. To reinforce their request, Confederate authorities imposed a ban on the shipment of Southern cotton to European factories, an action that was designed to demonstrate the reliance of a large segment of the European economy on this staple. The delegation was composed of William Lowndes Yancey, Pierre Adolphe Rost and Ambrose Dudley Mann. Yancey, Rost and Mann were unlikely choices for such a mission, and the general speculation was that these men were sent abroad in order to get them out of the way during the formative period of the Confederacy.

William Lowndes Yancey was a native of Georgia but had been reared in a New England antislavery home. By the early 1830s, however, he had become enamored with the idea of Southern nationalism, and on his return to the South, he became an outspoken advocate for preserving the institution of slavery and the creation of an independent Southern nation. His selection to a diplomatic mission to convince European nations to recognize the Confederacy is difficult to understand because antislavery sentiment was on the rise in these nations and Yancey's passionate endorsement of the institution was sure to offend the very persons he was trying to convince that the Confederacy deserved recognition without abandoning slavery.

The remaining two members of the delegation were political nonentities. Pierre Rost was a native Frenchman but had immigrated to New Orleans, where he taught school and studied law under Jefferson Davis's brother, Joseph. He was a slave owner and a member of the Louisiana Supreme Court. His connection to the Davis family probably accounted for his appointment to the delegation, but like Yancey, his ownership of slaves seriously affected his ability to influence the heads of European countries to grant recognition to the Confederacy.

Ambrose Dudley Mann, a Virginian by birth, had experience as a negotiator of commercial treaties for the United States and as a minister to smaller European states. He served as the first assistant secretary of state from 1853 until 1855. He cast his lot with the Confederacy in 1861 and was quickly appointed as a member of the delegation. His effectiveness as a Confederate diplomat, like that of Yancey and Rost, was negligible. He eventually was appointed commissioner of the Confederate States for

Pierre Rost, a native of France and a member of the Louisiana Supreme Court, was a member of the first Confederate delegations sent to Europe in a vain effort to secure diplomatic recognition of the new nation. *Courtesy of the Wynne Collection.*

Belgium and the Vatican. He remained in Europe after the war and died in France in 1889.

The original Confederate diplomatic mission to Europe was quickly replaced by a two-man delegation, consisting of James Murray Mason and John Slidell, in November 1861. The arrest of these two men aboard a British ship, *Trent*, by the USS *San Jacinto*, under the command of Captain Charles Wilkes, triggered a major diplomatic brouhaha with Great Britain that came close to war. Great Britain sent troops to Canada to reinforce its claims that its rights had been violated, and popular sentiment in the North demanded military action against the British. Lincoln and other Federal officials, recognizing the danger inherent in getting involved in such a war when they already faced a war with the Confederate States, released Slidell and Mason after a few weeks and offered an abject apology to Great Britain. The two Confederate diplomats were sent on their way, but the *Trent* affair, although settled diplomatically, severely damaged relationships between the two countries. Confederates hoped that the confrontation would result in immediate recognition of the Confederacy, but that was not forthcoming.

The quest for diplomatic recognition of the Confederate States as an independent nation dominated Southern foreign policy. There was much to be gained by such recognition—military assistance, loans and the legal purchase of arms and ships from European suppliers—which, while available secretly, would have greatly increased the chances of survival for the Confederacy. Interestingly, Great Britain did grant recognition of a state of belligerency between the United States and the Confederate States, which gave Confederate warships the right to access foreign ports for resupply and for protection. To some degree, the recognition was based on a legal error included in Lincoln's blockade proclamation that limited the Union blockade to Southern ports while international agreements recognized a blockade only if all of a nation's ports were closed. Thus, this limitation, some argued, was tantamount to tacit recognition of the Confederate States as a separate nation by the United States. An interesting legal point, perhaps, but one that eventually came to naught.

By mid-1863, the question of diplomatic recognition of the Confederacy became moot as the Union armies in the East and West secured major victories—Gettysburg and Vicksburg—that persuaded European powers that the South could not prevail. Additionally, Southern cotton, once vital to the factories of Europe, was gradually replaced by cotton grown in Egypt and India. Although these new cotton crops produced coarser fibers, European mills quickly adapted machines to use them and consumers readily accepted cloth made from them. By 1864, so much cotton had been warehoused in England that some was reshipped to mills in New England. Thus, at a time when Confederate armies were faltering, the death knell sounded for King Cotton diplomacy. European nations, faced with grain shortages for their people, were more interested in importing Union wheat than cotton, and commercial ties with the North strengthened as trade with the South weakened.

Only an increasingly unlikely failure by Federal armies in all theaters of operation would convince European nations to grant recognition of the Confederacy.

Chapter 2

Finding a Way

Whereas we are happily at peace with all sovereign powers and States:
And whereas hostilities have unhappily commenced between the Government of the
United States of America and certain States styling themselves the Confederate States
of America:
And whereas we, being at peace with the Government of the United States have declared
our royal determination to maintain a strict and partial neutrality in the contest between
the said contending parties:
We therefore have thought fit, by [and with] *the advice of our privy council, to issue this*
our royal proclamation:
And we do hereby strictly charge and command all our loving subjects to observe a
strict neutrality in and during the aforesaid hostilities, and to abstain from violating or
contravening either the laws and statutes of the realm in this behalf or the law of nations
in relation thereto, as they will answer to the contrary at their peril.
—*Queen Victoria, May 13, 1861*

In late 1861, Confederate president Jefferson Davis made one of the most important appointments to the Confederate cabinet when he selected a former United States senator from Florida, Stephen Russell Mallory, to serve as secretary of the navy. Mallory, whose appointment was opposed by some representatives from his home state, brought considerable experience in naval matters to the new nation since he had served as the chairman of the Senate Naval Affairs Committee. He was a competent administrator, a reliable supporter of the Confederate cause and an amiable soul who was

Stephen Russell Mallory served as the Confederate secretary of the navy and was responsible for creating a navy for a nation that had no ships and few experienced seamen. *Original drawing by Jeanette Boughner. Courtesy of the Wynne Collection.*

able to work effortlessly with difficult men. Although the Confederate navy was seriously underfunded, Mallory realized that Southern success depended to a great degree on being able to break the Union blockade of Southern ports, on preventing Union control of the Mississippi River and on creating a fleet of blockade runners that could bring in vital military supplies from Europe. With a small budget of only $15 million, he set out to do just that, but he could not do it alone. He needed to find men who shared his vision of the Confederacy as a naval power and who possessed the necessary skills to circumvent both the Federal blockade and the restrictions imposed by neutral nations.

James Dunwoody Bulloch, who was an agent for Fraser, Trenholm and Company in Liverpool, would become the most important man in Confederate naval service throughout the Civil War. A former officer in the United States Navy, he had left military service and entered private business. When war came in 1861, he offered his services to the Southern cause as a procurement agent in Great Britain. To that end, he had boarded a ship for Liverpool, using his business relationship with Fraser, Trenholm and Company—cotton factors—as cover. Although he did buy and sell Confederate cotton for British textile mills, he was a man on a different kind of mission for the Confederacy, and the niceties of diplomatic recognition, treaties or any other formal sanctions would not deter him.

Cotton easily converted into hard currency, and the Confederate War Department kept him supplied with the fiber, which had been purchased from Southern plantation owners or received in lieu of taxes. Quickly, word spread through Liverpool that Bulloch had money and was willing to spend it on war materiel of all kinds. Arms, ammunition, medicine and uniforms were bought and stockpiled in the warehouses of Fraser, Trenholm and Company, awaiting shipment to the South. In order to evade the Union navy, which blockaded the Southern coastlines, he utilized British ships—ostensibly neutral vessels— to ferry the contraband across the Atlantic, and when the United States exerted diplomatic pressure to shut down this operation, he found other carriers willing to run the risks of the blockade. He had also been the man behind the purchases of several steamships he had converted into warships and that now preyed on the vast commercial fleets of American companies. In November 1861, he had personally delivered the CSS *Fingal*, loaded with more than eleven thousand rifles, pistols and cannons and seven tons of shells, to Confederate authorities in Savannah.

James Dunwoody Bulloch, an uncle of Theodore Roosevelt, was the Confederate purchasing agent stationed in Liverpool. His bold purchases of ships and munitions made him indispensable to the Confederacy. Bulloch remained in Great Britain after the war. *Original drawing by Jeanette Boughner. Courtesy of the Wynne Collection.*

The greatest obstacle Bulloch faced in purchasing ships for the Confederate naval service was the Foreign Enlistment Act, which prohibited the construction *and* arming of warships in British shipyards for a belligerent power. Thus, most ship purchases by Confederates had to be disguised as commercial ships or as warships destined for other countries. Union spies plied the docks of Greenock, Scotland, and Liverpool, England, seeking information on Confederate ships, which they then forwarded to British officials with demands for action to prevent their sailing. British officials, hesitant to take action while the possibility of Confederate victory existed, pursued a policy of "looking the other way" until the Union successes at Gettysburg and Vicksburg in mid-1863. The CSS *Florida*, the CSS *Alabama* and the CSS *Atlanta* were early purchases, but their successes in damaging the American fleets brought the full weight of that country's diplomatic power and the threat of military action. Bulloch was forced into using subterfuges to circumvent the hard eyes of British customs inspectors. Ships he now purchased were built as merchant vessels and, upon completion, taken to Terceira in the Azores to be outfitted with weapons. He played a dangerous game but was delighted when one of his "illegals" took to the sea. Although the achievements of these cruisers were fodder for newspapers and raised the morale of the Southern population, they ultimately contributed little to the success of the Confederacy.

British shipyards, as well as those in France and Italy, were kept busy during the years from 1861 until 1865. Not only were Confederate purchasing agents active in buying finished ships and commissioning new ones, but European companies, particularly British ones, also were quick to place orders for fast, shallow-draft ships that could run the Union blockade. Without these small vessels, most of which were privately owned, Confederate armies would have been crippled because of a lack of ordnance, and the Southern people would have suffered more deprivation and hardships than they did. The Union navy, therefore, expended most of its efforts in preventing blockade runners from successfully entering Southern ports and leaving with cargoes of cotton, turpentine and tobacco that could be sold at high prices. Throughout the war, the cat-and-mouse game between blockaders and blockade runners continued. To this end, the Union commissioned 500 ships, which destroyed or captured about 1,500 blockade runners over the course of the war; nonetheless, 5 out of 6 ships evading the blockade were successful. In May 1865, the *Lark* became the last Confederate ship to slip out of a Southern port and successfully evade the Union blockade when it left Galveston, Texas, for Havana.

Northern shipyards kept pace as the Federal government moved rapidly to augment the number of ships available for blockade duty. The scarcity of available ships made the initial Union blockade porous, and Confederate naval ships and blockade runners slipped easily in and out of Southern ports, to the chagrin of Union diplomatic officials who were hard pressed to explain how the blockade was "effective" as required by international agreements. To offset the small number of ships available for blockade duty in 1861, the Union embarked on a vigorous shipbuilding effort to create almost one hundred "ninety-day vessels." These were small screw ships that carried a few cannons and a small crew. In addition, Federal authorities sent agents to various ports to purchase commercial ships that could be retrofitted for blockade duty. The Federal fleet was further augmented by captured blockade runners that were considered prizes of war. Still, not until mid-1863 were enough ships available to make the blockade truly effective.

The *Oreto* was built in Liverpool and was ostensibly built for the Italian navy. Purchased by James D. Bulloch, the ship's name was changed to the CSS *Florida*. From August 1862 until November 1864, the *Florida* wreaked havoc on Union commercial vessels on the high seas. *Courtesy of the U.S. Naval Historical Center.*

This October 18, 1862 depiction of the capture of British blockade runners reveals a source of ships for the Union's blockading squadrons, since many of these captured vessels were purchased by the navy and used in the blockade. Harper's Weekly, *October 18, 1862.*

The USS *Adela* was a fast side-wheeler that could keep up with the fastest blockade runners. Originally a British blockade runner, it was captured off Great Abaco Island by the USS *Huntsville* and the USS *Quaker City* on July 7, 1862. It was purchased by the Union navy and converted into a gunboat. *Original drawing by George H. Roger. Courtesy of the U.S. Naval Historical Center.*

To better utilize the small number of ships available to the Union, the Blockade Strategy Board, a joint commission of army and naval officers, was formed in June 1861 under the leadership of Captain Samuel F. Du Pont. The board developed two immediate objectives—taking control of major ports along the Atlantic Coast through combined army-navy campaigns and controlling other deepwater ports by stationing ships at the mouths of the harbors. In November 1861, Federal forces under the command of Du Pont seized control of Port Royal, South Carolina. The capture of this harbor provided the first blockading squadron a major base of operations, which with its repair and maintenance facilities ensured that Union ships could refuel without having to go all the way to Fortress Monroe. The earlier capture of Ship Island, off the coast of Biloxi, Mississippi, in September 1861 provided similar facilities in the Gulf of Mexico.

The southernmost city in Florida—Key West—remained in Union hands throughout the war and acted as the linchpin of the blockading efforts. With a fully functioning Federal court, Key West became even more important because captured Confederate ships and blockade runners were brought to the port to await adjudication. Because Federal crews were entitled to the funds generated by the sale of captured ships and their cargoes, the presence of such a court meant that sailors could receive their prize money more quickly. The court also fixed favorable prices paid by the Federal government for captured ships. Some of the captured blockade runners were repurchased by shippers who sent them back to blockade running. One such ship, a Spanish ship, was captured and sold three times. On the fourth capture, it was accidentally burned when a lantern overturned while the ship was being searched by the crew of the USS *James S. Chambers*.

Far from any of the settled areas of Florida, Key West remained impervious to Confederate attacks, since any land attack would have had to come from the mainland and no land route was available. The formidable guns of Fort Taylor and the lack of Confederate warships afforded the city protection from any naval attack.

Captain (later Admiral) Samuel F. Du Pont chaired the Union Blockade Strategy Board, which created the overall objectives of the United States Navy and carried out a survey of the Confederate coasts. Du Pont led the Union naval force that captured Port Royal, South Carolina, in November 1861. *Courtesy of the Library of Congress.*

Eventually, Key West would become a major headquarters for directing a portion of the blockading fleet.

When the blockade was first proclaimed by Lincoln, Flag Officer Silas Horton Stringham was placed in overall command of the Union effort, the Atlantic Blockading Squadron. Stringham quickly realized that such a task was too much for one person, and in September 1861, he retired from active duty. Although he was later promoted to rear admiral and recalled to serve as the commandant of the Boston Naval Yard, a post he had held previously, he did not participate further in the blockade operations. With the retirement of Stringham, the Blockade Strategy Board began subdividing the task of

The USS *Crusader* joined the Gulf Blockading Squadron in March 1861. It was typical of the screw steamers favored by Union captains during the war. *Courtesy of the U.S. Naval Historical Center.*

closing Southern harbors by creating more squadrons. By late October 1861, there were two squadrons—the Atlantic Blockading Squadron, based at Hampton Roads, Virginia, and the South Atlantic Blockading Squadron, based at Port Royal. A further division occurred when the South Atlantic Squadron was split again to create the Gulf Blockading Squadron, with responsibilities for patrolling the Gulf of Mexico from Key West to Mexico. This was the largest of the blockading fleets and it, too, was ultimately subdivided into the East Gulf Blockading Squadron and the West Gulf Blockading Squadron in early 1862.

The 1,500 miles of Florida's coasts became the concerns of the South Atlantic Blockading Squadron, which had responsibility for the Atlantic Coast from the extreme northern coast of North Carolina south to Cape Canaveral, and the East Gulf Blockading Squadron, which had most of the Florida coasts, from Cape Canaveral to Pensacola, as its area of operations. Each squadron encountered different problems, and each pursued different strategies.

Chapter 3

Florida Goes Dark

We the undersigned residents of Indian River, believing it a Solmen [sic] duty of every Citizen, to try and serve his State and Country in whatever capacity he may be most able, would in accordance to such feelings, report to your Excellency, that we have taken the responsibility of putting out the Lights at both Jupiter Inlet and Cape Florida, believing them to be of no use or benefit to our Government, but on the contrary of great importance to our enemies.

We had felt the importance of such a measure for some time, thinking some authorized Agent of our Government would be sent to perform it, but finding no effort was made by either the Government of the Keeper of the Light, we resolved to assume the responsibility ourselves, and report the result to your Excellency, hoping that it may meet your approval—At Jupiter we destroyed no property whatever, the Light being a revolving one and of very costly make, we took away only enough of the machinery to make it unserviceable—There is a quantity of property belonging to the Light consisting of Tools, machinery, Paints, oil &c which we have secured under lock and key.
—letter to Florida governor Madison Starke Perry, 1861

Florida was the third Southern state to declare secession, on January 10, 1861. At that time, Florida also had the smallest population of any state that would join the Confederacy. With a mere 145,000 residents—about equally divided between whites and slaves—the Sunshine State had little to offer in terms of men and materiel to the Confederate cause, although it would eventually become the South's major supplier of beef and salt. Population figures for the entire state showed that there was only an average population density of two persons per square mile, although this ratio changed to two to six persons per square mile in a swath that ran from the St. Johns River to Tampa. In the St. Augustine and Pensacola areas, the population was somewhat denser, averaging six to eighteen persons per square mile. In the plantation belt that stretched across north Florida, the population was densest, but even there, the heaviest concentrations accounted for only forty-five residents per square mile. As David Coles relates in one of his articles, Florida was "the smallest tadpole in the dirty pool of secession."

With secession, however, state officials immediately implemented a policy of preparing the state for the possibility of a war with the Union. The Chattahoochee Arsenal at Chattahoochee was seized immediately by state troops, while Florida troops also took control of Fort Marion at St. Augustine and Fort Clinch at Fernandina. These forts, which were occupied by small Union forces (Fort Marion had a single sergeant in residence), had little strategic value and were quickly retaken by Federal soldiers in early 1862 after the outbreak of war. Governor Madison Starke Perry, aware of how few stands of arms were available for Florida troops, went north seeking to

The Chattahoochee Arsenal, a Federal installation, was occupied by Florida troops immediately after the passage of an Ordinance of Secession in early January 1861. The guns and munitions stored there were issued to Florida troops. *Courtesy of the Florida State Photographic Archives.*

purchase arms, ammunition, uniforms and accoutrements for them. Within a few weeks, Floridians filled the ranks of state militia groups—many of which later became Confederate units—and the attention of military leaders turned to the navy yard and Fort Pickens in Pensacola.

In Pensacola, Union lieutenant Adam J. Slemmer had moved his small garrison from Fort Barrancas, one of the four forts in the area, into Fort Pickens. Despite demands from Confederate forces that he surrender the fort to them, Slemmer decided to hold out. For the next several months, Confederate batteries prevented the fort from being supplied or reinforced by Federal troops while a large Confederate army, under the command of General Braxton E. Bragg, held strategic positions in the city. Although unable to land, Union ships lay at anchor outside the harbor, effectively sealing the harbor.

Confederate troops continued to hold the installations on the mainland, and an unsuccessful attempt was made in October 1861 to take Fort Pickens. The two forces eyed each other across the harbor. Although a massive artillery duel took place in November 1861, the situation remained a stalemate until the Confederates decided to evacuate Pensacola in May 1862 and send their troops to join other units along the Mississippi River. Quickly occupied by Union troops, Pensacola remained secure under Federal control for the duration of the war.

There were Floridians who decided to take measures into their own hands and launched their own attacks on Federal property in the state. Paul Arnau, the customs officer at St. Augustine, organized a group of Southern sympathizers into a "coast guard" unit and set out to close the lighthouses along the Atlantic shore and thereby deny the Union navy assistance in capturing ships running the blockade.

The first light to be extinguished was the St. Augustine Lighthouse on Anastasia Island. Arnau and a woman, Maria De Los Delores Mestre, removed the lenses from the lighthouse and hid them. From St. Augustine, Arnau moved south to the Cape Canaveral Lighthouse, where Keeper Mills O. Burnham dismantled the lenses, crated them and buried them on his land near the Banana River. Whether he, a Northerner by birth, did so out of sympathy with the Confederate cause or because he was a loyal Unionist who wanted to protect the lenses from being destroyed is difficult to determine. The result was the same, however, and the lighthouse was dark throughout the war.

From Cape Canaveral, Arnau moved south along the Indian River Lagoon. At Jupiter Inlet, he found the lighthouse there still operating under the command of José Francisco "Joe" Papy, a loyal Unionist. Papy refused

The lighthouse at Jupiter Inlet was seized by James Paine and others, and the light and lenses were removed. The light remained closed throughout the war, denying blockading ships navigation assistance. Many of Florida's lighthouses suffered similar fates during 1861. *Courtesy of the Crankshaw Collection.*

to dismantle or even turn off the beacon. He said he was a Southern sympathizer but was paid to run the light and intended to keep his word to the Union government and the Lighthouse Service.

James Paine, a resident of the tiny village of St. Lucie north of Fort Pierce, decided the beam from the lighthouse could reveal blockade runners slipping through the Jupiter Inlet to the warships that patrolled offshore and inside the Indian River and St. Lucie River. He armed himself and walked south to the lighthouse, where he talked Oswald A. Lang and Francis A. Ivy, both assistant keepers, into doing their "patriotic duty." Along with Arnau, Lang and Ivy, Paine persuaded Papy to abandon the lighthouse and removed the operating mechanism and hid the parts.

From Jupiter Inlet, the group made its way to Key Biscayne, where they used a subterfuge to persuade the keeper, Simon Frow, to open the barred door to the lighthouse. Once again, the men removed important pieces of the mechanism that operated the light and damaged what they could not carry with them. Frow and his assistant were stranded on Key Biscayne to await rescue by passing Union ships. When his assistant deserted to join Confederate sympathizers in Miami, Frow was left to make his way to Key West and to report to Federal officials there.

Satisfied they had done what they could for the Southern cause, the men returned home. They reported their actions to Governor Madison Starke Perry and to Confederate secretary of war Christopher Memminger. Arnau, who had returned to St. Augustine, was taken prisoner by Union forces and held on a blockading ship until he revealed the location of the missing mechanism and lenses. August Oswald Lang, one of the partisans who darkened the Jupiter and Cape Florida Lighthouses, reportedly joined the Rebel army and then deserted. He was the first white man to live in what is now Palm Beach County.

On the western side of the Florida Peninsula, Confederate forces removed the mechanism from the lighthouse on Seahorse Key, opposite Cedar Key. Seahorse Key became a Union staging area, a prisoner of war camp for captured Confederates and a refugee camp for loyalists fleeing from depredations by their Confederate neighbors. Later in the war, Seahorse Key was used as a collection point for contrabands (slaves) fleeing their masters on the mainland.

At St. Marks, Confederate troops had removed the light from the lighthouse in order to prevent the lighthouse from aiding Union ships, which were patrolling the Apalachee Bay. St. Marks was a small coastal town, but during the antebellum period a small railroad had been built to connect it to Tallahassee and the surrounding tobacco and cotton plantations. Before the Civil War, St. Marks had established itself as the major port for exporting these staples to foreign and Northern markets, and it remained a favorite of blockade runners who could quickly gather full cargoes for their outward-bound dashes through the patrolling Federal ships. Local pilots who knew the bay had little need of the light, but Union commanders possessed only limited knowledge of shallow waters and depended on the light for safe passage.

Near the mouth of Tampa Bay, the lighthouse on Egmont Key had been rebuilt after an 1848 hurricane had made the original tower unsafe and had reopened in 1858 with a new third-order Fresnel lens. In 1861, keeper George V. Rickard found himself facing a dilemma. His superior, the customs collector in Key West, was loyal to the Union, while the customs collector at St. Marks sided with the Confederacy. Rickard pretended to be loyal to the Union when Federal blockading ships were near the island, but when they left the area, he decided to flee the island. After crating up the Fresnel lens, he fled to Tampa with the lens and as many supplies as he could transport. The lighthouse, however, was reactivated using a makeshift light when the blockaders returned.

Although the quick actions of Paine, Arnau, Rickard and others to deny Union ships the assistance of Florida's lighthouses were undertaken without specific orders from the Confederate government, their efforts were appreciated by the captains of the hundreds of small blockade runners that operated along both coasts of the Sunshine State. By 1862, the only operational lighthouses were those located south of Miami and westward to Fort Jefferson in the Dry Tortugas. Florida had gone dark.

Chapter 4

The Blockaders
A Sailor's Life

The sight of a woman had been denied us for eight long months, and we had only dim recollections of how they looked, and the sudden appearance of several of that sex upon our station, nearly prostrated us with astonishment and delight; and a general effort was noticed among all hands, to appear as attractive as possible in case the ship came near enough for the ladies to observe us. The officers hastened below to put on their best uniforms and arrange themselves generally for a conquest.
—*Israel Everett Vail, aboard the USS* Massachusetts, *1862*

In early 1861, the Union navy consisted of ninety ships, of which forty-two were commissioned for active service. Twenty-four of these were steam powered. By the end of that year, an additional seventy-nine steamers and fifty-eight sailing vessels had been purchased. The number of sailors had been increased from 7,900 in January 1861 to more than 24,000 in December 1861. By the end of the war in 1865, the Union navy had expanded to some seven hundred ships and an additional sixty ironclad coastal monitors. Of these ships, about six hundred were assigned to blockade duty along the Confederate coasts, with about four hundred on duty at any one time. The remaining ships were assigned to various overseas stations tracking and attacking Confederate commerce raiders. At any one time, approximately 86 percent of the total Union naval strength was devoted to enforcing the blockade. When the war ended in 1865, the Union navy reported some 51,000 sailors and officers on duty and a total of more than 132,000 men having served for some period of the war.

Blockade duty was considered to be the dullest and most tedious job in the Union navy. Sailors were often aboard ships for long periods of time with few opportunities to relieve their boredom except for the periodic returns to their home bases to re-provision or to take on coal. Supply ships, most often water carriers and mail ships, did provide some respite from the day-to-day tedium that was the life of the average sailor, but rendezvous with these ships were of a short duration. Initially, blockading ships returned to Hampton Roads, Virginia; Key West, Florida; and later Ship Island, Mississippi, to replenish their coal bunkers. Although the acquisition of Port Royal as an additional base in 1862 shortened the distances between bases somewhat, most of the sorties by blockaders lasted several weeks to a few months, a situation that contributed to the low morale aboard ship.

Despite the recognition that life aboard a blockading ship would be dull, more than fifty thousand men volunteered for blockading duty. There were several reasons for this, not the least of which was the tremendous amount of money that could be made while serving. A private in the Union army made a mere thirteen dollars a month, but a sailor on blockade duty had the chance to share prize money from the sale of captured blockade runners and their cargoes. Prize money could boost sailors pay to (for then) astronomical figures.

In July 1862, for example, the USS *Magnolia* captured the blockade runner *Memphis* as it attempted to run a cargo of cotton from Charleston. In September 1862, a prize court in New York sold the ship to the United States Navy and its cargo of cotton to Northern cotton mills for the whopping sum of $510,000, half of which was divided among the crew. In 1864, the crew of the USS *Aeolus* managed to capture the blockade runner *Hope* outside Wilmington, North Carolina's harbor. When the ship and its cargo were sold, the captain of the *Aeolus* was awarded $13,000; the chief engineer received $6,700, while each member of the crew was given $1,000 as his share. Even the cabin boy received $533. Although significant sums then, when the prize money is converted to today's dollar values—a factor of fourteen times as much—the amount is unbelievable. Of course, not all prizes were sold for such huge sums, but the chance for becoming a wealthy man was always present, and stories about such awards were prominently displayed on the pages of Northern newspapers.

Living conditions on board a blockader were not ideal, but they were much better than those endured by soldiers in the field. Discipline was vigorously enforced, and the limited confines of a ship meant that punishment for infractions was quick. Disciplinary action might be as light as extra duty assignments and loss of privileges or as stringent as imprisonment in the

The USS *Memphis* was originally a blockade runner and was captured in July 1862 with a cargo of cotton valued at $510,000. When the ship and its cargo were brought before a prize court and sold, the captain and crew shared half of the sale price. The U.S. government purchased the vessel and converted it to a blockader. *Courtesy of the U.S. Naval Historical Center.*

ship's brig, flogging or the loss of prize money. Charles K. Mervine, a sailor aboard the USS *Powhatan*, noted in his diary that two sailors who had gotten drunk and missed reporting for duty while on liberty during a stopover in Havana were confronted by the deck officer when they returned to ship. One of the men tried to strike the officer but was taken prisoner before he was able to inflict any physical damage. A court-martial was held on the *Powhatan*, and both men were convicted. Sentencing was withheld until the ship reached its home port of Key West two weeks later. Both men were sentenced to one year of hard labor, forfeiture of all pay due and the loss of pay during the year of servitude. One of them, who had accrued $2,000 in prize money, lost that money as well. The second was also dishonorably discharged from the navy at the end of his sentence.

Excessive drinking was a common problem aboard blockading ships. The Union navy, like its British counterpart, issued sailors a daily ration of grog, and officers were provided navy "sherry" to drink. On board the USS *James L. Davis*, Bosun's Mate Charles Williams reported an attack on his person, which resulted in the threat by the ship's captain to "suspend the men's grog ration for one month if another such incident took place." Earlier in May, the ship's executive officer reported that he had been unable to perform an assigned task "on acct. Of part of the launch's crew getting drunk at night while I was asleep." Alcohol consumption by Union sailors, bored by the humdrum daily life aboard ship, became such a problem that the daily allotment of grog was suspended on September 1, 1862. Federal sailors received a five-cents-a-day increase in pay to compensate them for their loss.

Simply prohibiting alcohol consumption did not stop sailors from seeking liquor from other sources. One ship's captain wrote in his log that only officers would be allowed to search the captain's quarters on captured vessels because most sea captains kept a supply of liquor in the cabins. Lieutenant John West, the captain of the USS *James L. Davis*, placed several crew members in irons for stealing a supply of liquor and getting drunk. The liquor belonged to the captain of the blockade runner *Isabel*, which the *Davis* had captured off St. Marks, Florida, on September 24, 1862.

Sutlers on private vessels that approached Union ships with fresh food and other goods would sometimes carry liquor in tin cans, which were labeled as oysters or canned meats. Although an ingenious way to market alcoholic beverages, these attempts to circumvent the navy's prohibition of strong drink were never enough to slake the demand for liquor. At every port of call where they were given shore leave, sailors would buy bottles of liquor and attempt to bring them back on ship. Some efforts were successful, but the smuggled supply never matched the demand. When officers discovered a sailor drinking or drunk, he was usually placed in leg irons and thrown into the brig. Other captains took a more active role in trying to suppress alcohol consumption by subjecting drunks to a continuous spray of salt water until they were sober.

Naval officers, well aware that idle hands made for trouble, scheduled daily activities to ensure that sailors stayed busy. Mondays were typically given over to washing clothes and practicing general quarters routines, such as running out the ship's large guns and shooting targets. Tuesday was the day for overhauling and repairing the ship's rigging, followed on Wednesday with small arms drills. Thursday was likely devoted to practicing emergency drills, such as firefighting. Friday was dedicated to scouring, scrubbing and polishing the decks and brass finishes in preparation for the captain's Saturday inspection. Saturday afternoons were set aside to make and repair items of clothing. Sailors were given the opportunity to attend religious services on Sunday mornings, while the afternoons were free time. Sailors engaged in a variety of pastimes during periods of leisure. Checkers, cards and music were favorites, although gambling was the favorite activity of some sailors. Carving wooden whimsies and other articles also provided an outlet for the men. Virtually any distraction was used to relieve the overwhelming boredom of blockade duty.

Occasionally, pursuits of blockade runners relieved the tedium of being on station. Seldom was there ship-to-ship combat—so little, in fact, that one historian has estimated that the total time given over to naval battles by ships on blockade stations was little more than one week out of the four years the blockade operated. Few blockade runners carried heavy armaments since cannons and heavy guns tended to slow down ships and dramatically increase their need for deeper water. Using heavy guns also demanded trained personnel to man them, and since most blockade runners were crewed by British civilian sailors, the prospect of combat made it difficult to find enough crewmen willing to take a chance. Perhaps the deciding factor, however, was that carrying heavy guns restricted the amount of space that could be used to carry saleable cargo. Blockade running was a commercial enterprise, and the owners of the vessels wanted nothing that would interfere with their ability to make a profit.

Although chases might be exciting, Union sailors on blockade duty had little to fear from combat on the water. Of the 132,000 men who served during the war, the Union navy lost approximately 5,000 men. Of these, 2,112 were killed in action or died as a result of wounds. Nearly one-fifth of the fatalities were scalded to death by burst boilers. Another 3,000 died of other causes, but total deaths still amount to less than 4 percent of the navy's wartime personnel.

As the blockade became better established, ship commanders began to send details ashore to destroy fortifications, conduct reconnaissance or meet Union sympathizers. As George Buker points out in his *Blockaders, Refugees & Contrabands: Civil War on Florida's Gulf Coast, 1861–1865*, such excursions could and did produce casualties—deaths and wounds from gunfire. Along Florida's Atlantic and Gulf Coasts, ships of the blockading squadron began to concentrate on the destruction of salt making operations, many of them protected by small detachments of Confederate troops. With each raid, the overall number of casualties increased, but compared to the casualties inflicted in land battles fought between the Confederate and Union armies, the number was miniscule.

Disease proved to be the greatest danger to Union sailors, whether serving on the blockade ships at sea or in vessels that supported Union army units along the rivers and estuaries where they encountered Confederate troops. In January 1861, the Union navy could count on the services of only 61 surgeons, 25 passed assistant surgeons and 45 assistant surgeons. At the end of 1861, 41 percent of these medical officers had left the service. The need for ships' doctors forced naval authorities to conduct a hurried, but effective, recruitment campaign. By 1864, the number had increased to 463 physicians available for service on the six hundred Union ships, most of whom (56 percent) were civilians who had been recruited to serve on a contractual basis or had volunteered for naval service. In addition, riverine vessels included navy personnel who were assigned medical duties.

Most Union ships included a doctor or surgeon as part of their crews, and medical problems—the most common illnesses were malaria, yellow fever, dysentery, scurvy and sexually transmitted diseases—occupied much of their time. In addition to these diseases, ships' doctors had to contend with the psychological disorders brought on by long assignments on station and the interminable boredom that dominated ship life. One of the most vexing afflictions sailors suffered from was a condition known as "land sickness," a terrible urge to smell the earth and to breathe air far removed from the ocean. There was little physicians could do, but sometimes a change of scene and some days ashore solved the problem. For some sailors, however, this uncertain treatment produced little in the way of results, and when their despondency led to real illnesses, they had to be sent home.

Scurvy, which had largely disappeared in the American navy in the mid-1840s, made a virulent reappearance among sailors of the blockading fleets. In 2001, Frank R. Freemon, the author of *Gangrene and Glory: Medical Care during the American Civil War*, stated uncategorically, "By 1860, scurvy had disappeared from the American navy." Just a year later, Alfred J. Bollett, the author of *Civil War Medicine: Challenges and Triumphs*, called scurvy an "ongoing problem" for the Union navy since long periods on station and a reliance on salted and canned foods deprived sailors of the vitamin C found in fresh vegetables and fruits. On October 11, 1862, Admiral J.L. Lardner, who commanded the East Gulf Blockading Squadron, reported to Union secretary of the navy Gideon Welles, "The terms of enlistment of the *Kingfisher's* crew having expired for some time, and symptoms of scurvy prevailing among them, I have ordered the commander of that vessel to Boston, and to report to the Department upon his arrival."

The USS *Midnight*, which operated off the coast of Texas in 1861, reported "forty cases of scurvy and dysentery," which effectively took it off station and out of action for a short time. In all, the Union navy reported more than five thousand cases of scurvy during the four years the blockade was in place.

Although sailors on duty on blockading ships could be certain that they could escape the horrors of the large battles and massive casualties soldiers experienced on land, they could not escape the ravages of deadly diseases.

Chapter 5
The Blockade Runners' Friend
Yellow Fever

SIR: In my letter of June 19 (Nos. 195, 196) I stated to the Department that indications had forced me to the conviction that we were to have a season of yellow fever at this port. My worst fears have been more than realized, and for more than two months the disease has held its course without abatement and is now as virulent as at any time. The season of epidemic lasted in 1862 nearly till the 1ˢᵗ of November, and there seems no reason to believe that it will disappear sooner the present year, except it shall have exhausted all the material for disease before that time.
—Rear Admiral Theodorus Bailey, East Gulf Blockading Squadron, Key West, July 27, 1864

The most damaging diseases were yellow fever and malaria, which devastated entire crews and took ships off station. These were diseases that proved to be deadly to land armies as well. During the course of the war, the Union army alone recorded 1.3 million cases of malaria, which resulted in 10,000 deaths. Statistics for the Confederate side were similar. Both diseases are initially transmitted by mosquitoes and have many symptoms in common. Often the terms "yellow fever" and "malaria" were used interchangeably to describe the same disease, so much so that the term "yellow fever" was used exclusively in reporting outbreaks to naval authorities. Exposure to low, swampy areas and to stagnant water increases the likelihood of becoming infected. As Union sailors ventured on land or as ships approached the mainland, they frequently encountered huge swarms of mosquitoes and suffered outbreaks of these diseases as a result.

Little was known about the cause of yellow fever, and even less was known about the methods (vectors) of transmitting it. Quarantine was used to combat the spread of the disease, and infected sailors were ordered to their beds until they either died or recovered from its effects. Quinine, which proved to be an effective treatment for malaria, was in great demand during the war. Blockade runners often carried large quantities of quinine in the cargoes because the drug brought high prices on the open market in Southern states. Blockading ships experienced severe outbreaks among their crews, necessitating their removal from duty. So prevalent was yellow fever on Union ships of the blockade that in December 1862, Fleet Surgeon G.R.B. Horner recommended the abandonment of Key West as a

> *place of rendezvous for the squadron in summer, 24 vessels of the Navy and the merchant service having been infected with the fever in the harbor within the last five months, including the* James L. Davis, *the last infected. According to report yesterday, she has had 16 cases since she left here last month, making 18 with 2 cases left by her in the marine hospital, and of the former 2 have died. Should she continue infected, I would recommend that she likewise return to a Northern port in the coming spring.*

Admiral Theodorus Bailey forwarded the surgeon's request to Gideon Welles, although he disagreed with Horner's suggestion that Key West be vacated during the summer: "I can not agree with him about Key West as a rendezvous or depot."

The experience of one Union ship, the USS *James S. Chambers*, under the command of Acting Master Luther Nickerson, demonstrates how the disease might be contracted and its impact on the operation of a ship. In June 1864, Admiral Theodorus Bailey, the commander of the East Gulf Blockading Squadron, assigned the *Chambers* the task of patrolling the east coast of Florida and of stopping the activities of small blockade runners in the area. It was standard naval practice to anchor a blockade vessel off an inlet and send in longboats with armed men to reconnoiter the long Indian River lagoon and seize any blockade runners found inside. The men also burned any homes or facilities that might be found, although the area technically was uninhabited. The practice of longboat raiders originated with Lieutenant Commander Earl English of the USS *Sagamore* and parties led by a Southerner turned Yankee raider, Acting Master's Mate Henry A. Crane. The *Chambers* arrived on station off the Indian River Inlet on July 15, 1864. The ship's log records the quick progress of the disease among the crew.

The summer in Florida was no different then, except for clouds of mosquitoes that often carried the dread disease yellow fever and for which no methods of control existed. On July 18, Nickerson put his longboats into the water and sent them into the Indian River and Jupiter Inlets with orders to camp overnight, watch for blockade runners and then return. He could not have known how fatal his orders were. His men found no human enemy but battled their way through clouds of stinging mosquitoes.

The *Chambers* floated just offshore in the heat and rain, its crew beset by the stinging insects. On July 19, the first case of yellow fever was reported on the ship. Unfortunately, the victim was the ship's medical officer, Acting Volunteer Surgeon F.J. Williams. The medical log kept by Williams shows him treating men for routine shipboard problems on the previous day, and then no further entries are made until October.

On July 21, Nickerson sent Acting Master's Mate J.F. Van Nest and five armed men into the Indian River Inlet with supplies enough for a one-week expedition. The next day, July 22, in a report written to be transported to Admiral Bailey, Nickerson recorded, "Yellow fever has been reported among the crew." Then he added, "But there have as yet been no deaths." Two men were ill. There would soon be deaths. There is no explanation for the reason Nickerson decided not to remove his men from the inlet and sail north, according to the policy. Log and message books and official correspondence give no hint of the reason he stayed in the area.

Nickerson may not have wanted to abandon his duty station. He might have hoped to capture more blockade runners so his crew could enjoy a larger share of prize money. The only hint of his thoughts, the line saying there had been no deaths, seems to show he was hopeful nothing more would happen. On July 25, with the surgeon still too ill to function, the *Chambers* stopped and boarded the schooner *Aristides* bound for Key West from Port Royal, Jamaica. They found the crew heavily infected with yellow fever and handed over some medicine. On board the *Chambers*, three of its crew members were ill, including the surgeon.

On July 28, the longboats found twenty refugees on the shore of the Indian River. "Refugees" was a term used by the navy to describe either people sympathetic to the Union and seeking refuge or acting as armed raiders for the Union. The logbook does not give details as to women and children, so this group was probably one of the irregular bands fighting against Southern militia and the famed "cow cavalry" that herded cattle from Florida to Southern forces in the battle zones.

The July 29 logbook entry notes, after detailing the weather and what the crew was doing, that the number of men down with the fever had grown to nine. The number dropped to five by July 31, but the surgeon was still too ill to perform his duties, so officers and crew members cared for the sick as best they could. The remainder of the crew continued with their normal duties. Longboat crews went in and out of the inlets and endured unending assaults by mosquitoes and other biting insects. The crew drilled at the guns and exercised the ship at general quarters.

And the sick list started creeping up. "Six men reported with fever," noted the log entry for August 2. On August 3, the log entry notes that sixteen men were now suffering from the fever. The remaining crew of the *Chambers* found it difficult to carry out the normal routines of the ship, and two men who had been confined to the brig—Henry Reeves and Peter Kelley—were released because their services were needed to work the ship.

By August 4, the sick list included twenty-two crewmen down with the fever. The next day, the first death occurred when F.J. McCann, paymaster's steward, died. Five additional men were listed as suffering from the fever in the ship's log. "Fever increasing" was the note entered by J.A. Shaffer, officer of the deck for the fourth watch. McCann was buried at sea with full military honors. His was the last full military ceremony, for fever was now raging through the ship and there were not enough men able to carry out the job.

On August 6, Leading Seamen Joseph McCloskey and Thomas Hardin died. There were twenty-nine of forty-five remaining crewmen and officers on the sick list. Once again, J.A. Shaffer made a note in the ship's log: "The threatening appearance of the weather and debilitated state of the crew compelled the burial of Thomas Hardin and Joseph McCloskey at sea; which took place at 9:30 a.m." He added, "Fever increasing."

There were thirty-one men ill with the fever on August 7, and the names of three more were added on August 8. That left only fourteen men and officers to work the ship, man the guns and nurse the sick. The *Chambers* was out of action without having fired a shot along the Indian River. They had not seen a blockade runner or another Union vessel since August 5.

Nickerson did not have enough able-bodied seamen to man a gun, operate a longboat or bury the dead in a proper military fashion. The bodies were just loosely wrapped and dropped over the side into the Atlantic Ocean. On August 9, he wrote his next-to-last official message to Admiral Bailey in Key West:

> *I regret to be compelled to report that since my last communication the sickness on board this vessel has assumed the form of a most malignant fever and increased to an alarming extent. To-day* [sic] *we have a sick and binnacle list of 38, over two-thirds of our number. Three of my officers were taken last night and are very sick. I have lost four men to death since the 5th Instance, burying one this morning (First Class Boy William*

Wilkinson). There are a number of others I have but little hopes of. The few remaining who are not sick are worn down by nursing the sick. I can barely raise enough men to man a boat. I do not think it is yellow fever, but never saw persons suffer so much and become so reduced in such short time. The symptoms are much the same as that disease.

Nickerson had no way to send the message. He had to wait until a ship passed close enough to see his signal for help. Late in the day an army vessel, *Transport*, saw his signal, stopped, passed over some medicine and took Nickerson's message to Bailey in Key West.

Although the ship's surgeon, Williams, had recovered enough to work, he faced a ship full of patients, many on the verge of death, and few sailors to call on for help. Then Nickerson came down with the fever and could no longer command what was left of the crew.

On August 10, crewmen Able Seamen Harry L. Simmons, Leading Seaman James Halkyard and Fireman H.G. Chace died and were buried at sea with perfunctory rites.

The litany of death continued in the logbook entry for the next day:

August 11, 1864, Thursday, off Indian River, Fla. At 2 a.m., Joseph Stebbins, quartermaster, died of the fever. At 7:30 a.m. buried the remains of H.G. Chase, fireman, and Joseph Stebbins, quartermaster at sea. At 1:30 p.m., Alex Wertts, leading seaman, died of the fever and was buried at sea. At 8:45 p.m., Hiram Cripps died of the fever. Sick list 30. Acting Mate William C. Underhill, the only deck officer in good health was standing all watches and performing all the funeral ceremonies.

It was the same on August 12. Michael Gleason and Henry McKenzie, gunners, died and were buried at sea. Two officers—William Eldredge, an acting ensign, and Acting Mate Robert B. Rodney—returned to duty to help Underhill, who was by now much fatigued. Very little changed the next day when, on August 13, Acting Master's Mate J.F. Van Nest, who had recovered from the fever and now commanded the *Chambers*, wrote in the log, "Up to the morning of the 13th instant we lost 12 men and one officer." On that day, Acting Ensign Henry E. Hopkins died and was buried at sea.

Later that day, a ship was sighted coming from the south. It was the USS *Honeysuckle*, a steam tug sent by Admiral Bailey to assist the *Chambers*. Acting Ensign Eldredge described what happened next in a report he wrote to the secretary of the navy:

A steamer hove in sight, coming from the southward. At 9 a.m. proved to be the U.S. Tug Honeysuckle. *Came to anchor at 10:45 a.m. and brought a doctor and medical stores and 8 contrabands* [slaves who had fled from their masters] *from Key West borne on the books of the Naval Storekeeper there.* [They were] *Peter Wiggans, Edward Reese, Charles Grandy, William Henry, Henry Harrison, Moe Hopkins, Andy Horne, Stan McDonald.*

Consultation of officers, Acting Ensign William Eldredge, and Lt. Cyrus Sears, the Honeysuckle *captain, as well as Passed Apprentice Surgeon Macomber. It was decided the* Chambers *was unable to keep blockade and should sail north. At 3.20 p.m. got under weigh* [sic] *and stood to the northward. Eldredge in command.*

But the dying wasn't over. The medicines and the ice brought by the *Honeysuckle*, which returned to Key West for fuel, were ineffective in stopping the fever outbreak. On August 14, an able seaman named Slavin died and was buried at sea due east of present-day Vero Beach.

On August 15, Nickerson died and was buried at sea. His death was the last straw for Surgeon Williams, and Acting Ensign Eldredge wrote in his report, "At 1:15 A.M. Surgeon F.W. Williams was seized with nervous debility and insanity—brought on by over exertion, anxiety and attention to the sick, for many days." Williams wrapped himself in the anchor chain and jumped overboard to his death.

There was one last tragedy before the ship reached port in Philadelphia. Eldredge reported that off Cape Hatteras at 6:15 p.m. on August 18, "Acting Master's Mate John F. Van Nest in, it is supposed, a fit of derangement jumped overboard and was drowned, in spite of every effort made to save him: vessel hove too, boat lowered, buoy thrown overboard, etc. This was in Latitude 35.1 Longitude 75.10."

The unfortunate *Chambers* was replaced by the barkentine *James L. Davis* in the Indian River. The war and the blockade would go on. In Philadelphia, the *Chambers* was refitted, given new officers and crew and then transferred to the blockading squadron off South Carolina. Near the end of the war, it became a quarantine ship at Port Royal, once again caring for yellow fever victims.

The experience of the *Chambers* and its ill-fated crew was unusual, but other ships operating along the mosquito-infested coasts of the Sunshine State experienced minor outbreaks. Towns frequently experienced outbreaks of yellow fever as well. Fort Myers, Tampa and Key West suffered outbreaks of yellow fever. In June and July 1864, Key West was devastated by the disease and the entire crew of the USS *Wanderer*, which had been recalled to that city

Admiral Theodorus Bailey commanded the East Gulf Blockading Squadron from his headquarters in Key West. Admiral Bailey held that post from November 1862 until August 1864, when he fell victim to yellow fever. *Courtesy of the U.S. Naval Historical Center.*

for duty as a hospital ship, fell victim to the disease and one crewman died. Yellow fever was no respecter of rank. In early August, Admiral Theodorus Bailey, the commander of the East Gulf Blockading Squadron, contracted the fever and boarded the USS *San Jacinto*, whose crew was also suffering from yellow fever, to head north to New York Harbor for quarantine. His temporary replacement in command, Captain Theodore P. Greene, soon fell victim to the fever, and Commander R. Hanson relieved him. Major General Daniel Phineas Woodbury, the Union army commandant in Key West, likewise fell victim to yellow fever and died on August 16. The headquarters for the East Gulf Blockading Squadron was moved to Tampa pending the end of the fever epidemic. In September, Commodore C.K. Stribling was appointed to replace Admiral Bailey, and the squadron's headquarters were reestablished in Key West.

Most official reports to Secretary of the Navy Gideon Welles revealed only occasional references to the outbreak of disease, but prior to his departure, Admiral Bailey wrote a long report to Secretary Welles detailing the extent of the spread of yellow fever among the ships of his squadron:

> [T]*he yellow fever has been raging at this post with a violence that has exceeded that of 1862, or I believe of any previous year. The vessels that have been detained here perforce have suffered severely. The steamer* Nita *was under repairs that rendered it impossible for her to get away. Every person on board but two officers has been taken ill of the fever and so far some ten or more have died. On the ordnance ship* Dale *I believe every person has been taken excepting Commander Handy and a boatswain's mate. The executive officer, Acting Ensign Joseph A. Denman, the master's mate, Robert Wisner, Acting Master Miller H. Johnson (on board under arrest), and Surgeon's Steward Purcell, the*

only officers excepting the commanding officer living on board, were taken and all died. I lost also four of the barge's crew who were on board, and others of the Dale*'s crew also died. The* Wanderer *had but three men; all were taken; one died; the others are in a critical condition. The guard schooner* Eugenie *has also lost perhaps one-fourth of her men. On shore the sickness and mortality have been even greater. The provost-guard of 45 men has lost more than half its number, and the mortality among the citizens and refugees has been alarmingly great…Meantime, in spite of every effort, the fever has manifested itself on several of the vessels. The* Huntsville *has had from 20 to 30 cases. Her sick list for to-day shows 14 cases, and those assuming a more malignant type than the previous ones. I can spare this vessel as well now as a fortnight hence. A portion of her shaft is being forged at New York and must be nearly ready, so that a week or two sooner or later is not of importance, as she would necessarily go north to receive the machinery. I am, however, very sorry to part with the* Merrimac. *I am advised, however, by the surgeons, and my own observation of the nature of the disease and its intensity, this season confirms their advice, that unless the vessel goes north every person on board will in all probability have the disease and very many must necessarily die. I have therefore concluded that in the interests of humanity the vessel should be sent north. She has lost so far but one officer—Acting Third Assistant Engineer Thomas Cunningham—but several of them are now sick, there being at present 8 cases in all, as appears by the surgeon's report enclosed with another communication on this subject.*

The other vessels in which the disease has appeared are the Honduras, *the* Iuka, *the* Marigold, *the* Honeysuckle, *and the* San Jacinto. *Deaths have occurred of officers and men on these vessels. When I last heard from the* San Jacinto *she had had but four cases, of which but one had terminated fatally—that of Lieutenant Tecumseh Steece, who died at sea on the 15th of July.*

Despite the long list of ships unable to continue on blockade duty, Bailey assured Secretary Welles that "the blockade of this coast shall be preserved at all events, whatever the sickness. The squadron is much crippled, and its cruisers that have served to break up in so great a degree the commerce between Mobile and Havana, but the coast is as thoroughly blockaded as at any previous time and the squadron as effective to prevent all egress and ingress."

Bailey's assurances proved correct, and the blockade continued in place. The fever outbreak in 1864 was only a momentary setback to the Union navy's efforts to blockade the ports of Florida and their efforts to prevent blockade runners from circumventing it. Still, it is easy to understand why one historian called yellow fever "the blockade runners' friend."

Chapter 6

For Patriotism and Profit
Blockade Runners

Scarlett: But you are a blockade runner.
Rhett: For profit, and profit only.
Scarlett: Are you tryin' to tell me you don't believe in the cause?
Rhett: I believe in Rhett Butler, he's the only cause I know. The rest doesn't mean much
to me.
Dialogue, Scarlett O'Hara and Rhett Butler
—Gone With the Wind *(MGM Pictures), 1939*

With the proclamation of a blockade of Southern ports in 1861, questions about its legality and effectiveness were raised. William Lowndes Yancey, a member of the first Confederate delegation to Europe, informed the British government that during the first three months of the blockade, more than four hundred ships had entered and left Southern ports, a point that was made again by James Mason and John Slidell. By the end of 1861, Mason, along with William Lindsay, a member of Parliament, argued that the number of ships successfully running the blockade had increased to more than seven hundred. Despite these arguments, the British government, at the urging of the foreign secretary, Lord John Russell, recognized the blockade as legitimate in February 1862.

Although skeptical of its effectiveness, the British government and Prime Minister Lord Palmerston, who concurred with Russell's assessment, made their decision based not on facts but on their desire to avoid a war with the United States. Just a few months earlier, the two nations had come perilously close over the *Trent* affair—so close, in fact, that the British government had sent eleven thousand troops to Canada and mobilized the thirty thousand members of the Canadian defense force in December 1861. That same month, British warships scouted Southern ports for evidence that the Union navy had sealed Southern ports to commerce, but the captain of the sloop HMS *Desperate*, which cruised into the harbor of Galveston, Texas, reported that he had seen no Union blockaders in the area and "I concluded the port was not effectively blockaded and it will be my duty to report the same to my superior officer." Across the South, British diplomatic officials reported the same. In Charleston, the British consul reported no significant decrease in commerce and so, too, did British consular officials in New Orleans, Savannah and Wilmington. In August 1861, the consul in Charleston described the Union blockade as "the laughing stock of the Southern Merchant Marine." Certainly, the large numbers of commercial ships moving in and out of Southern harbors made it seem so.

Jochem H. Tans, in his article "The Hapless Anaconda: Union Blockade 1861–1865," points out that any impartial evaluation of the blockade, based on the statistical data compiled by earlier historians Frank Owsley and Marcus Price, proves that it was a psychological success but a practical failure. Of all the vessels that attempted to run the blockade—some 6,316—an amazing 85.3 percent were successful. Fast steam-powered ships, plying coastal waters, enjoyed the most success, completing 92.1 percent of their attempts, or an amazing 2,526 out of 2,743 times. The 3,573 attempts made by slower sailing vessels succeeded four out of every five times (80.2 percent) they made runs. The costs to the United States to construct, buy or convert captured ships to police the blockade were enormous and far outweighed the value of confiscated cargoes or destroyed blockade runners.

The success of blockade runners was critical to the success of Confederate armies in the field. When the war started in 1861, the number of available stands of small arms for use by Confederate soldiers numbered only 300,000, not enough to equip the 325 regiments of infantry and 35 regiments of cavalry raised in Southern states during 1861. So scarce were arms for troops that Southern armies began the practice of policing battlefields and collecting discarded arms for reissue to troops newly arriving to reinforce units or to new units formed to expand the size of the Confederate armies. Although Southern industries tried desperately to create factories capable of meeting the needs of the armies, they failed throughout the war. In order to carry on the war, it was absolutely necessary to receive arms from European nations. In April 1861, Captain Caleb Huse and later Major Edward C. Anderson were dispatched to Europe to purchase the needed equipment. Their efforts were in addition to the activities of other agents who, under the direction of James Bulloch, were busily scouring the arsenals of Europe for armaments.

The blockade runners were the answer to the Confederacy's problem of finding sufficient quantities of arms to fight a war. From 1861 to 1865, some 600,000 stands of arms were imported, together with 3 million pounds of lead. Large quantities of field artillery, cloth and leather for uniforms and 2.5 million pounds of saltpeter—a critical ingredient in the manufacture of gunpowder—were brought in by ships brazenly challenging the Union blockade. One historian estimated that over 60 percent of the modern arms in Confederate service found their way through the leaky sieve of Federal blockaders. Without the determined efforts of the blockade runners— whether motivated by patriotism or profit—the Confederate army would have been unable to sustain any kind of large-scale or extended campaign against the Union. The war would have ended quickly, if not quietly, in 1861.

Despite the success of blockade runners, there was a constant problem of supplies for the Confederate armies. The large profits to be made supplying consumer goods to wealthier Southerners and the limited funds available to

The blockade runner *Teaser* was typical of the British-built blockade runners that successfully challenged the Union blockade. Usually painted gray with one or two raked smokestacks, such vessels had a shallow draft and side wheels that would allow them to enter blockaded ports through narrow creeks and inlets. *Courtesy of the U.S. Naval Historical Center.*

the Confederate government meant that the majority of the cargo space on blockade runners was devoted to satisfying the demands for silks, wines and other luxury items. Although various Southern states and the Confederate government tried to operate blockade runners on their own, the loss of a single ship could effectively bankrupt a state budget for such activities or seriously restrict those of the central government. The self-imposed embargo on the export of cotton and other Southern staples exacerbated the problem. Although both the state governments and the Confederate government attempted to mandate the allocation of a portion (50 percent) of each blockade runner's cargo space be set aside for arms, munitions and equipment imports, enforcement of this requirement was difficult. Even when private runners successfully made their way into Southern ports with munitions, they charged exorbitant prices for the military supplies they carried, and Confederate officials had no choice but to pay what was asked.

Blockade running was profitable for private owners—so much so that companies were formed in Britain for the sole purpose of taking advantage of the high prices Confederate citizens were willing to pay for scarce items. Philip Van Doren Stern reported that such companies often paid 500 to 1,000 percent dividends to investors in this "golden bonanza." Although about 1,500 blockade runners were captured, the loss of a ship and its cargo had little impact on profits because most operators were willing to pay high premiums for insurance against losses.

Stern demonstrates the enormous profits that could be made by a single successful run to and from a Southern port:

PROFITS AND COSTS
SUCCESSFUL BLOCKADE RUN
ROUNDTRIP

Costs

Wages (Officers and crew)	$18,840
Food (passengers and crew)	5,700
Coal, oil	5,800
Insurance, pilot fees, miscellaneous	12,625
Risk Insurance	37,500
Total Expense	$80,465

Earnings

800 bales of government cotton	$40,000
800 bales of privately owned cotton	40,000

Return freight for owners	40,000
Return freight for government	40,000
Passenger fares	12,000
Total Earnings	$172,000
Profit	$91,535

Although companies made money on transporting Southern cotton, the real profit came when they bought cotton in Southern ports and resold it in Britain. The staple sold for as little as six to eight cents a pound when it sat on Southern docks but could bring as much as twenty-five cents to a dollar a pound in Great Britain. By the end of the war, so much cotton had been brought through the Federal blockade that British mills had a surplus of 500,000 bales. Some 200,000 of these bales were then transshipped to textile factories in the United States. For whatever its value as an instrument of war to the Union, no one could seriously doubt its value to private investors. Stock in blockade running companies not only paid high dividends, but it was often resold for two or three times its initial value.

British investors, sensing a great opportunity for high profits, poured as much as $250 million into building new ships with low profiles and

The USS *Fort Donelson* was the former blockade runner *Robert E. Lee*. It is almost identical in size, shape and engineering to the blockade runner *Teaser*. *Courtesy of the U.S. Naval Historical Center.*

shallow drafts, combined with powerful steam engines that could achieve a top speed of eighteen to twenty knots at sea. Ships employed an early version of stealth technology. Usually painted a dull gray to blend in with the ocean water and blue skies, the runners burned anthracite coal, which produced little smoke that was almost white in color. Once these ships neared the Southern port of choice, they usually waited until dark before making runs to the shore. Running lights were doused, sounds were muffled and crews went about their tasks silently. The same techniques were used to exit. Blockading Union ships, usually constrained to operate in deeper waters outside harbor channels, were frequently surprised to see new ships at anchor when the sun came up.

British runners arrived at Southern ports from different directions. Halifax, Nova Scotia, was an unlikely port to start a run south, but between 1861 and 1865, an estimated forty-six ships made a total of eighty-five runs through the heavily patrolled Northern coastline to deliver cargoes to the Confederate ports of Wilmington, North Carolina; Mobile, Alabama; and Charleston, South Carolina, to bring Southern products back. Despite repeated efforts to close them by the Union navy, Charleston and Wilmington remained important centers for blockade running for most of the war. Although the Union navy had the use of Port Royal, South Carolina, as the headquarters of the South Atlantic Blockading Squadron and a growing number of Union blockading ships, the numerous small rivers and inlets leading into the Carolina harbors proved impossible to blockade entirely.

Mobile's harbor remained open because of the protective fire of the cannons of Fort Gaines and Fort Morgan at the mouth of Mobile Bay. Mobile was closed in 1864 when a massive invasion fleet commanded by Admiral David Glasgow Farragut stormed past the forts, fireboats and torpedoes to take control of the port and the Tombigbee, Tenasaw and Mobile Rivers, which were used as transport routes into the heart of the lower Confederate states. As late as mid-1864, there were twenty-two attempts by steam-powered blockade runners to reach Mobile, and of these, nineteen were successful, and none of the steam vessels was captured exiting the port.

Nassau, Bermuda, Matamoros and Havana were other favored destinations for British blockade runners, which used the facilities of these neutral harbors to make repairs and refuel. Often, cargoes were offloaded into warehouses, where they were stored until transferred to smaller coastal steamers or sailing vessels for runs into blockaded harbors or along the coasts of Florida. Although some of the larger British blockade runners managed to successfully breach the blockade and proceed directly to Wilmington, Mobile and Charleston, their principal role was to serve as bulk transporters delivering cargoes that would be broken up for transshipment in smaller vessels.

Matamoros, Mexico, which shared the mouth of the Rio Grande River with Brownsville, Texas, was also a favorite destination for British runners. It was not unusual for as many as two hundred ships to be in the harbor at any one time. Cargoes could be offloaded in Matamoros and simply ferried across the Rio Grande into Brownsville. From there, Confederates could ship them north to Houston and, at least until mid-1863, thence across the Mississippi River into the heart of the Confederacy. When Union forces gained complete control of the Mississippi, small sailing vessels and coastal freighters moved the cargo in small increments to the hundreds of small bays and inlets along the coasts of Texas, Louisiana, Mississippi, Alabama and Florida.

The South did not have a strong tradition of commercial shipping, nor did it possess secure shipyards where runners could be built. As a result, British runners relied on crews and officers recruited from experienced personnel of the British navy. Typically, a British captain would take leave from the navy, agree to captain a blockade runner, recruit a crew and, after loading a tightly packed cargo of several hundred tons (packed so tightly, it was said, that "a mouse would have no room to hide"), depart for Bermuda, Halifax, Havana or Matamoros. Salaries for crews were high. A captain might earn several thousand dollars, paid in gold and half paid upfront, for each successful trip, many times the average annual salary he earned in the Royal Navy. Pilots familiar with the waters around blockaded ports who could bring ships through the cordon of Union ships were also highly paid. Crewmen could earn several hundred dollars for the same trip. Bonuses were usually awarded at the completion of a run, which boosted salaries even higher. There were few vacancies on blockade runners.

Although blockade runners were instrumental in supplying the basic needs of Confederate armies, armaments and medicines were not the most profitable items to carry in their holds. The people of the South demanded and willingly paid for the importation of luxury items—silks, perfumes, millinery, books, fine liquors and exotic wines and hundreds of other nonessential items. For example, Hiram Smith Williams, a private in the Fortieth Alabama Regiment fighting against General William T. Sherman's army on the road to Atlanta, was able to acquire books published in England within a few months of their original publication date. One merchant in Wilmington is reported to have asked his agent in the Bahamas to stop sending so much chloroform and instead send "essence of cognac." Zealous Confederate patriots accused blockade runners—whom they charged with profiteering on luxury items while Southern soldiers suffered deprivations and scarcities of even the most basic food and clothing—of being traitors to the Southern cause. The truth was, however, that blockade runners took great risks and brought in items the public demanded. The fact that runners were willing to devote one-third to one-half of their cargo space to critically needed equipment for the Confederate government mitigated this harsh judgment somewhat. In defense of blockade runners and the enormous profits they gained, one historian points his finger at the "many women in the back country [who] flaunted imported $10 gewgaws and $50 hats as patriotic proof that the 'damn Yankees' had failed to isolate them from the outer world."

Jochem H. Tans places the blame for the deprivations and shortages suffered by the Confederacy's citizens and soldiers not on the shoulders of profiteers but on the inability of the Southern government to take advantage of the weaknesses in the Union blockade and on the South's lack of industry. Without the profit motive spurring private investors to risk capital on ship construction and personnel, the blockade running activities would have been miniscule at best, leaving Southern armies without enough munitions to fight an extended war. Without blockade runners, the American Civil War probably would have lasted no more than a few months.

Chapter 7

Florida's East Coast in the Blockade

The Atlantic ocean washes Florida on the east, from the Bahama channel to the S.E. angle of the territory. The ocean line, is composed of a border of islands, narrow and low, with intervening channels, which are generally shallow and impeded by bars of sand. The Atlantic tides are very unequal and irregular on the coast of Florida, from which circumstance great inequality [of depth] *must be found on the bars at different seasons.*
—*William Darby,* Memoir on the Geography, and Natural and Civil History of Florida, *1821*

The northern Florida ports of Fernandina, Jacksonville, St. Augustine and New Smyrna were assigned to the South Atlantic Blockading Squadron headquartered in Port Royal, South Carolina. Fernandina and St. Augustine were occupied by Federal troops by late 1861, and Jacksonville was occupied and abandoned four times by Union forces over the course of the war. The activities of the Union army, combined with the activities of the Federal navy in and around these ports, quickly eliminated them as viable destinations for blockade runners.

New Smyrna, on the large and shallow Mosquito Inlet, however, became an important port for the myriad small sailing ships and coastal steamers that made their way through the cordon of Union ships patrolling the coast. With its proximity to the St. Johns River, New Smyrna was a favored port for shipments of military equipment that could then be carried overland and redistributed through the network of interior rivers of Florida. With a

This Federal picket boat came under fire by Confederate sharpshooters hiding in trees along the riverbank, circa 1863. *Courtesy of the* Jacksonville Times-Union.

stone dock that provided a secure facility to offload or load cargoes, the small town flourished as small runners brought in thousands of stands of arms, medicines and luxury items. In addition, bales of cotton and thousands of running feet of Florida pines and oaks were collected for transportation on outward-bound runners. Hundreds of small saltworks surrounded the small village, and the salt—more valuable per ounce than gold—produced by them made its way to the interior for transshipment north. More than two thousand blockade runners found the complex system of rivers, bays and marshes provided sanctuary from the ever-present Union ships that prowled the shores of the barrier islands that protected the town.

The USS *Penguin* and the USS *Henry Andrew* maintained a constant presence in front of the village, although they were hamstrung in stopping the small vessels that regularly visited the port. In March 1862, the blockade runner *Kate* delivered a cargo of six thousand Enfield rifles, ammunition, shoes and medicines to Mosquito Inlet, destined for Confederate armies near Corinth and Iuka, Mississippi. The eyes of the Confederate nation were focused on this small Florida port. So, too, were the watchful eyes of Union sailors.

Crude sawmills harvested Florida pines and oak trees for export through the blockade. This sawmill could produce thousands of running board feet of Florida timber monthly. *Courtesy of the Florida State Photographic Archives.*

On March 22, six longboats filled with men from the two ships, seeing the determined efforts of local residents to move the piles of equipment to safety beyond the town, made their way toward New Smyrna. Unknown to the raiders, Confederate troops assigned to guard the shipment prepared an ambush. As the Union sailors neared, the Confederates opened fire with rifles and an artillery piece. The commanding officers of both ships, plus several crewmen, were killed. The raiding party retreated, and both ships left the area.

Unfortunately, local civilians and the members of the Third Florida Infantry Regiment, which had been assigned to protect the valuable cargo, plundered the supply of shoes and rifles. Along the route inland, more guns were simply appropriated by local troops. One officer, according to some reports, sold guns, ammunition and medicines from the shipment and put the proceeds in his pockets.

Governor John Milton assured Confederate authorities that the pilfered equipment would be recovered and dispatched Captain Alonzo B. Noyes to trace the convoy's route and gather up the stolen items. Throughout

April and most of May, Noyes made a valiant effort to retrieve the lost rifles and supplies. Although he was successful in recovering most of the weapons, some remained, along with most of the shoes and other supplies, lost forever.

Although the Confederate government's experience with the *Kate* cargo left a bitter taste in the mouths of officials and a reluctance to route future cargoes through the port, New Smyrna became one of only three ports—Wilmington and Charleston being the other two—that remained open to blockade runners.

Governor John Milton, a staunch supporter of the Confederacy, tried to keep the pilfering of smuggled goods to a minimum. Milton was a popular governor, although his efforts to keep cotton from exiting the Sunshine State through the blockade in 1861 aroused the ire of wealthy cotton producers and speculators. *Courtesy of the Florida State Photographic Archives.*

In July 1863, Union vessels attempted to close New Smyrna by shelling the town. Lieutenant Commander Earl English, who led the attacking force, reported to Admiral Theodorus Bailey on August 12:

> *On the afternoon of the 28th I attacked New Smyrna with the U.S. dispatch steamer* Oleander *and schooner* Beauregard *and boats belonging to this vessel and the schooner* Para, *which vessel was stationed off blockading that place. The* Oleander *took the* Beauregard *in tow, crossed the bar and anchored abreast the place giving it a good shelling, the boats going up past the town. We captured one sloop loaded with cotton, one schooner not laden; caused them to destroy several vessels, some of which were loaded with cotton and about ready to sail. They burned large quantities of it on shore, which we could not prevent. Landed a strong force, destroyed all the buildings that had been occupied by troops. In landing the party was fired upon by a number of stragglers concealed in the bushes. The conduct of all connected with the expedition was most praiseworthy.*

There were no Union casualties.

Northern newspapers sent artists and reporters into every theater of war, including the blockading fleets. This artist depiction of Union sailors firing at a schooner trying to run the gauntlet of Union ships was published in *Harper's Weekly* in 1864. *Courtesy of the Wynne Collection.*

Although New Smyrna was in the patrol area assigned to the South Atlantic Blockading Squadron, that fleet was busy conducting an assault against Fort Sumter and would remain occupied with that task for the next year. Despite the success of this raid, New Smyrna continued to operate as a port for blockade runners.

The long Florida coast between Cape Canaveral and Key Biscayne contained no operating ports during the war. Present-day Titusville, then known as Sand Point, was the only village between the cape and the small village of Miami on Biscayne Bay. Census records indicated that fewer than five hundred persons lived between the two villages, a stretch of about 350 miles. There were no ports or harbor facilities available, and the coast was much the same as William Darby had described it in 1821.

Although few permanent residents made this long coast their home during the war, the absence of people actually worked to the advantage of blockade runners. The Indian River, a shallow 155-mile non-tidal lagoon screened by a continuous barrier island, provided shelter for the small sailing runners that ran regular routes between Nassau and the Florida coast. The wide, flat beaches fronting the ocean were ideal for landing such craft and unloading small cargoes. The narrow barrier island allowed for the rapid movement of the contraband to the Indian River, where waiting boats would ferry it to the mainland or up the lagoon to Sand Point. Once a cargo reached Sand Point, it would be transported overland to the St. Johns, moved downriver to the Ocklawaha tributary and from there into the interior of the state. Although the cargoes were small and contained mostly consumer goods—medicine, coffee, salt, needles and liquor— they also frequently included small arms and munitions.

Florida's East Coast in the Blockade

Small steamers, like this one on the Ocklawaha River, plied the tributaries of the St. Johns River, ferrying the cargoes of successful blockade runners into New Smyrna to markets in the interior of Florida. *Courtesy of the Wynne Collection.*

The eastern coast of Florida also included a number of small rivers and creeks, along with small bays, where illicit cargoes could be unloaded and either started along the inland supply routes or hidden until they could be retrieved later. Acting Master's Mate Henry A. Crane, assigned to the USS *Sagamore* and commanding small boats often sent into the Indian River Lagoon, reported to his commanding officer, Lieutenant Commander Earl English, in February 1863 the fruits of his forays into the Indian River:

> January 18.—*Found 4 bales of cotton at or in St. Lucie River.—Found three several parcels of salt, 41 sacks (130 bushels), near Jupiter, and destroyed them. I detached a party of five men on the morning of February 3 to Jupiter Narrows, who succeeded in finding 4 bales of cotton and bringing with them 2; they reached us last evening late.*
> February 7.—*Found two casks, partly filled with sperm oil, near this place, and 47 sacks of salt, one boat sail, etc.*

Crane was the bane of smugglers on the Indian River and a most unlikely foe for blockade runners. He came to Florida from New Jersey to fight in the Second Seminole War. When his army enlistment expired, he settled in St. Augustine and married in 1837. Over the next nineteen years, he and his wife, Sophia, had one son and six daughters. When the Armed Occupation Act was passed in 1842, Crane moved to a place not far from modern-day Sanford, in what was then Orange County. In 1844, Governor William D. Mosley named him a probate judge for Orange County.

But Crane did not stay there. He moved to Tampa and became a printer for the *Tampa Herald*. Later, he became a photographer when the profession

Along the Indian River Lagoon, the few settlers in that 155-mile stretch of isolated Florida frontier lived in crude huts or cabins and eked out a subsistence living. Blockade runners would often hide their cargoes in this wilderness and retrieve them later when the threat of Union gunboats was gone. *Courtesy of the Florida State Photographic Archives.*

Acting Master's Mate Henry A. Crane led boat crews from the USS *Sagamore* on raids up and down the Indian River. Crane was a disaffected resident of Tampa who joined the Union navy and attacked blockade runners. He was later made an officer in the Second Florida Cavalry and led raids against Confederate cattle drives. *Courtesy of the Crankshaw Collection.*

began as ambrotype photography. This was an early form of photography that used glass plates mounted on a dark background so as to appear as a positive image. When the Third Seminole War (1855–58) broke out, Crane volunteered and was commissioned a lieutenant. After the war, he returned to his trade as a printer and photographer until the outbreak of the Civil War.

Crane, then forty-seven, at first was regarded as too old to fight and joined a militia organization, the Silver Grays, to defend Tampa in 1861. He was given the rank of lieutenant colonel of militia and later turned down a commission at the same rank in the Confederate army. Then something happened. It may have been the murder of a friend from the Second Seminole War, John Whitehurst, a Union sympathizer, at the hands of Confederate guerrillas. Crane asked authorities to prosecute the killers, but they refused.

Disgusted at what he saw as a miscarriage of justice, Crane resigned his commission and left with two other men, James Henry Thompson and Levi S. Whitehurst. They walked across the state along the trail from Fort Brooke to Fort Capron just north of present-day Fort Pierce, near the Indian River. Once on the Treasure Coast, Crane met two other men, James Armour and a man known only as "Mr. Hall." The five men went to the Indian River Inlet, where they found two other men whose names have not been recorded, set up a camp and waited for a Federal blockade ship to appear.

On October 27, 1862, the USS *Sagamore* appeared offshore and sent in a longboat in answer to Crane's signals. The *Sagamore's* captain, Lieutenant Commander Earl English, recorded in his logbook that he had picked up "seven refugees at the Indian River Inlet." Any Southerners picked up along the coast by blockade vessels were recorded as "refugees" if they were pro-Union or as "Rebels" and "prisoners of war" if they were Confederate sympathizers.

On board the *Sagamore*, Crane outlined a plan to travel up the Indian River to Sand Point (present-day Titusville), cross over to the St. Johns River and capture a Confederate blockade runner and bring it down the St. Johns to Jacksonville. English said he had no authority to launch such a mission and would take the seven men to Key West to meet the commander of the blockading squadron. Before the *Sagamore* left the waters off the Treasure Coast, it captured the British steamer *Trier*, sank two sloops that went down with all hands and then headed for Key West.

Admiral Theodorus Bailey, commander of the South Atlantic and West Gulf Coast Blockading Squadrons, liked Crane's plan and had him sworn in as a volunteer acting master's mate. His partners were sworn in at lesser ranks, and all were attached to the *Sagamore*. Making the men members of the navy, the admiral said, would prevent them from being hanged as traitors if they were captured. Pursuant to the approval of Bailey, English issued an order to Crane on January 3 to "proceed with the party under your command, capture and run the steamer down to the mouth of St. Johns River, and then deliver her and report yourself and party to the officer commanding blockade at that place. Should you not find it practicable to run her down the river, you will burn her, bringing with you the valves and eccentric strap, and return to this place with your party, capturing any vessels you may see on your way down Indian River."

Crane depended on Armour to navigate because he was familiar with the Indian and St. Lucie Rivers. On the evening of January 3, 1863, Crane and his associates got into a longboat and went through the Jupiter Inlet and into the Narrows. Thompson became ill, reducing the strength of the raiding party, but Crane pushed on northward until suddenly he confronted another boat coming south. Crane's men drew their weapons faster, and the other boat surrendered. Crane had captured the crew of the schooner *Pride* that had brought in 188 bushels of salt. He dumped the salt into the river and took the *Pride* as a prize. He went back down the river to the inlet. As he headed south, he saw two men hiding on shore. He sent his crew ashore and took them prisoners.

The *Sagamore* had moved north, but the schooner *Gem of the Seas* was on station and took the prisoners. The ship's surgeon said Thompson was too ill to proceed, and Crane was given some regular navy men to complement his forays into the rivers.

On January 8, the *Sagamore* seized the British sloop *Julia*, ten miles north of the Jupiter Inlet, while Crane and his men rowed inside the inlets. The next day, Crane captured two more men in a rowboat and then found the unmanned schooner *Flying Cloud*, of Nassau, Bahamas. He burned the schooner because he did not have enough men for a prize crew. Besides, a storm was raging offshore.

While Crane waited inside the inlet, the *Sagamore* helped rescue troops and crews from the troopships *Lucinda* and *Sparkling Sea*, which had been driven aground south of the Jupiter Inlet during the storm. All the men were saved, but the horses the ships were transporting to a cavalry unit were lost.

On January 12, Crane found a cache of supplies including sailcloth, 150 gallons of oil and almost two hundred bushels of salt hidden near the Jupiter Lighthouse. He destroyed the materials and moved up the Indian River. Once the materials were destroyed, Crane and his party continued their northward journey on the Indian River.

The apparently indefatigable Crane did not spend much time resting. One wonders about his zeal for the Union cause because his son, Henry

Lafayette Crane, was fighting for the Confederate army with the Fourth Florida Infantry. This split loyalty apparently had no impact on his work, and he continued his foray along the Indian River.

Traveling north on the lagoon, Crane found a woman, Mrs. Isaiah Hall, and her six children. He took them to the Indian River Inlet, made them a camp and then signaled for the *Sagamore* to pick them up. On February 22, Crane and his men found a Confederate shipyard hidden in a cove north of the Indian River Inlet on what is now called Blue Hole Creek (modern maps show this place just south of the St. Lucie/Indian River County line on Hutchinson Island). He reported that the shipyard had repair supplies and a dock and that workers could see Union vessels sailing along the coast, but those vessels could not see the shipyard. Crane destroyed the facility by burning it.

He traveled as far north as he could and went into the St. Sebastian River, going five miles upstream. There he found a schooner hiding. He decided to hide near the Indian River Inlet and watch the vessel's crew bring it downriver until he was sure the ship was headed for the Jupiter Inlet. When the schooner sailed south on the Indian River in the dark, he maneuvered his longboats in the narrows, where he set a trap. Crane and his men hid their boats in the shadows of the shoreline and waited until the schooner came so close that they could hear the crew talking.

Surprise was complete, and they found they had taken the schooner *Charm* under Captain James Titus of Nassau. As they headed toward the Jupiter Inlet, they found a sloop loaded with cotton but unmanned. Crane put some men aboard the second vessel, and both sailed to the inlet. Eventually, custody of the two ships and the prisoners was transferred to the *Gem of the Seas*, which was standing offshore. The transfer of the men and ships to the *Gem of the Seas* resulted in a minor dispute between the captain of the *Gem*, Acting Lieutenant I.B. Baxter, and the *Sagamore*'s captain, English. On March 6, Baxter sent a report to Admiral Bailey stating emphatically that, in his opinion,

> *The* Sagamore *has no claim on them as they were captured during her absence from this station, and turned over to the U.S. bark* Gem of the Sea *by Mr. H.A. Crane two days previous to the* Sagamore's *arrival off here. I also respectfully beg to say that in my opinion the* Gem of the Sea *is entitled to the credit of the capture of the above prizes instead of the* Sagamore, *although Mr. Crane and his party were not regularly transferred to the* Gem of the Sea; *still I deemed them as a portion of her crew, in the absence of the* Sagamore, *as we had them to look after and to furnish with provisions the greater part of the time for the last two months;*

nor do I think they could have remained in Indian River during the absence of the Sagamore *without the protection of the* Gem of the Sea, *which vessel has not been absent from this station since the 30th of December last.*

Bailey's decision on the dispute is not known.

Under the rules of the Union navy at the time, captured enemy vessels were sold at auction and the crew that captured them received a good part of the proceeds. Crane, whose seizures of ships and property inside the Indian River enriched the members of the blockade fleet, was a popular man and well regarded by his commanders. He was becoming wealthy, and so were the officers over him.

His mission to the St. Johns was never completed by Crane because his activities on the Indian River took up his time. The *Sagamore*, with Crane and his men, left the Treasure Coast and went to Key West to rest and refit and returned in April in time to sink the British sloop *Elizabeth* and all hands just off the Jupiter Inlet on April 18. Crane went back into the river but found nothing to capture.

The situation improved for the *Sagamore* in June when the ship captured the English sloop *Clara Louisa*, plus three schooners—*Southern Rights*, *Shot* and *Ann*—all trying to enter the Indian River and Jupiter Inlets. Then Crane's days on the river ended, and the *Sagamore* was sent into the Gulf of Mexico to serve there.

Crane's service to the Union cause in Florida did not end with his adventures as part of the *Sagamore*'s crew. He would surface again as a captain in the Refugee Rangers, a mobile unit made up of volunteers and troops from the Second U.S. Colored Infantry Regiment. Still later, he would accept a commission as captain in the Second Florida Cavalry (Union) and participate in the Union's attack on the port of Tampa.

The East Gulf Blockading Squadron was very active along Florida's Atlantic Coast throughout the war. A cursory examination of the *Official Records* reveals that between 1862 and the end of the war in 1865, 47 blockade runners—sloops, steamers and small transports—were captured or destroyed by the Union fleet patrolling the area from Cape Canaveral to Jupiter Inlet. Additional ships were captured or destroyed between Jupiter Inlet and Key West during the same period by the squadron. If, however, the estimates of successful runs made by vessels through the blockade (85.3 percent) are correct, more than 250 ships escaped detection or capture and destruction. However, even this limited success by the Union blockaders had a telling blow on the Southern economy and on the ability of the Confederate military to supply its troops.

Chapter 8

Florida's West Coast in the Blockade

Fort Myers to Bayport

I can only say that no exertion has been wanting on my part to make the blockade as effective as possible with the force at my disposal, but I have never had a sufficient force of suitable vessels—sailing vessels being of little value to blockade steamers, especially when their draft of water is such as to prevent their lying close in, and in places where the current runs at the rate of three or four knots an hour, as it does off Mobile and the Mississippi River.
—*William W. McKean, flag officer, commanding Eastern Gulf Squadron, April 3, 1862*

The same ships and men that patrolled Florida's eastern shores also performed the same duty on the state's western shores. Transfers of men and ships from east to west were coordinated by the commander of the East Gulf Blockading Squadron from his headquarters in Key West. Each patrol area presented different problems and demanded different actions. Operations along the west coast included coordinated attacks inland by naval and army personnel, something that happened only occasionally on the east coast.

Fort Myers, located at the mouth of the Caloosahatchee River (sometimes referred to as the Sanibel River), was the southernmost town along the east coast. The river, which arose about seventy-five miles in the interior of the state, had provided a valuable route for United States troops in search of warring Native Americans in the Seminole Wars of the antebellum period. While Fort Myers remained little more than a frontier outpost in the years after the end of the Seminole Wars, nearby Punta Rassa, which also shared the mouth of the Caloosahatchee, became a thriving, if small, shipping point for thousands of Florida cattle each year. The periodic influx of large herds, destined for markets in Cuba, brought ships from various nations to Punta Rassa. The use of Punta Rassa as a shipping point continued for several decades after the Civil War.

North of Punta Rassa and Fort Myers, Charlotte Harbor offered ships a large and protected anchorage. The Peace River, which flowed into the harbor, emanated from the center of the state, where small settlements, such as Fort Meade, were located. The river also provided a highway from the Gulf to the central part of Florida, which, along with the Charlotte River, would prove to be important to blockade runners during the war. Screened by barrier islands, Charlotte Harbor (sometimes referred to as Gasparilla Sound) became an important outlet for the shipment of Florida cattle north to Confederate armies. Jacob Summerlin, a Confederate supporter and cattle baron, favored the small port of Punta Gorda for this purpose, although he also conducted long trail drives overland with herds destined for the railroads in southern Georgia.

Still farther north along the Gulf Coast was Tampa, the second-largest town in south Florida after Key West. The large open entrance to Tampa Bay was difficult for the Union navy to effectively patrol, and its shallow waters easily accommodated the small coastal steamers and sailing vessels used by blockade runners. The Hillsboro River, which emptied into the bay, pointed straight to the heart of Confederate Florida, and a network of prewar roads made the transport of smuggled goods easy. A small contingent of Confederate troops protected the harbor with small arms and cannon batteries. Union ships that ventured into the heavily used portions of the estuary were subject to furious fusillades from shore.

Bayport (also referred to as Bay Port), located on the mouth of the Weeki Wachee River, was founded in the early 1850s as a port to export cotton and citrus from plantations and farms in Hernando County. The river was short—only seven and a half miles long—but it provided easy access to the more heavily populated plantation district in central Florida. When Union blockaders intensified their efforts to close the larger ports on the west coast of the state, Bayport became the preferred port for the small steamers and sailing ships that could and did operate in the shallow coastal waters. Not only did Bayport offer such ships the natural protection of shallow water, but Confederate Home Guards also manned a battery of two cannons that provided additional protection against Union blockaders. Between 1862 and 1865, several artillery duels were fought between blockading ships and Rebel batteries. Several small skirmishes were fought between Union troops that tried to close the port and Home Guards that were determined to keep it open for business.

Two other small rivers north of Bayport—the Homosassa River and the Crystal River—were also used by runners to load cotton, turpentine and citrus for their outward trips and to bring in small shipments of arms and luxury items. During the years from 1862 to 1865, the East Gulf Blockading Squadron intercepted more than a dozen runners approaching Bayport or the other rivers, but for each ship captured, three or four made it through the blockade.

The blockading squadron paid little attention to Punta Rassa and Charlotte Harbor during the first eighteen months of the blockade, although several small vessels were captured making their way through the channel at Boca Grande and near Sanibel and Captiva Islands. The primary focus of the Union fleet during 1861 and 1862 was curtailing the flow of inward and outward runners from the major ports of Tampa, Cedar Key, Apalachicola and St. Marks. By 1863, however, the East Gulf Blockading Squadron possessed enough ships on duty to tighten its patrols and to pay more attention to smaller entrepôts visited by small steamers and sailing vessels. On February 2, 1863, the schooner *Two Sisters*, which served as a tender for the USS *St. Lawrence*, reported the capture of the sloop *Richards* in the channel near Boca Grande carrying a cargo of salt, coffee, liquors and shoes.

Like the barrier islands of the east coast, the barrier islands that fronted Punta Rassa, Punta Gorda and Charlotte Harbor offered some protection against the probing eyes of the blockading squadron, but the deeper channels and numerous passes made it easier for the squadron to pursue runners. Sanibel, Captiva, Cay Costa, Useppa, Boca Grande and Pine Islands offered ideal beaches for small sloops and schooners to load or unload cargo. On March 7, 1863, Luther Nickerson, acting master of the schooner *James S. Chambers*, reported to Admiral Theodorus Bailey in Key West that "information has reached me from sources that I deem reliable that there are numerous small craft trading along this coast in this immediate vicinity, especially about Punta Rasa [*sic*] and up the Sanibel (Caloosahatchee) River. There are many islands between this place and Punta Rasa [*sic*] that afford the facilities of landing cargoes unobserved." That same day, Nickerson reported the capture of the Spanish sloop *Relampago* by two armed boats from the *Chambers* on March 3 as it attempted to enter the harbor at Fort Myers. Like the *Richards*, the *Relampago* carried a cargo of coffee, liquors and soldiers' shoes. In the same report, Nickerson describes the capture of the schooner *Ida*:

About 4 p.m. on the 4th instant, while lying by the sloop taking off some of the men, a sail was reported to the south of us, standing in for the land; I left the sloop in charge of Mr. Smith and went in chase of the sail, which proved to be a schooner, When within a mile and a half I threw a shot across her bow, which she did not regard, but continued her course for the beach (distant about 2 miles) without showing any colors. I continued the chase, firing at her, until she was beached. A few moments after she struck, men were seen running for the woods, leaving her with her sails set. She was beached about midway of Sanibel Island, 15 miles to the south of this place. I came to anchor about 1½ miles from her, and waited for the sea to become smooth enough to land in order to save or destroy her cargo. The following morning I sent boats on shore and found her bilged. She was a small schooner of pilot-boat build; had hailed from Key West; she had the name of Ida *on her stern, but her place of hailing painted out. We took several boat loads of her cargo, which consisted principally of liquors; we set fire to her and left her.*

Charlotte Harbor and Punta Gorda, which had earned excellent reputations as cattle shipping ports before the war, continued to play important roles in sheltering blockade runners arriving to offload cargoes and as staging areas for collecting cargoes for outward-bound runners. The Peace River, often referred to as Peace Creek, and the Myakka River allowed small runners to find safety out of the harbor and away from raids or shellings by Union blockaders. With a depth of eighteen feet, Charlotte Harbor was rated the second-best harbor on the lower half of Florida's Gulf Coast, behind Tampa Bay, which had a depth ranging from fourteen to twenty-one feet. The Cedar Keys, which was the western terminus of the Florida Railroad, had an overall depth of nine and a half feet. In his instructions to Union captains in 1861, Flag Officer William Mervine, the first commander of the then consolidated Gulf Blockading Squadron, described Charlotte Harbor and Tampa Bay as having "facilities for entering and navigating [which] offer fine opportunities for commerce, and which must some day doubtless be connected with the railroad system farther north; at present they are scarcely used." Cedar Keys, which had received the first engine and cars on the Florida Railroad just weeks before the outbreak of the war, was already connected to the interior of the state, and according to Mervine, "The connection with Fernandina by railroad gives Cedar Keys its chief importance."

The Tampa–Cedar Keys route presented potential problems to Union blockaders. In August 1861, Lieutenant T. Augustus Craven, who commanded the USS *Crusader* and surveyed the potential ports on the west coast of the Sunshine State, warned Flag Officer William Mervine that "there is an inshore channel from Tampa to Cedar Keys through which communication is kept up, and which can only be effectually destroyed by the destruction of the settlement at Cedar Keys and the breaking up of the railroad there. Most of the buildings at that place belong to the Government, having been put up by the army. The same may be said of the Tampa settlement."

Early on, the Union navy established a coaling and watering station on Egmont Key, slightly to the north of the entrance to Tampa Bay. The heavy use of this facility provided almost continuous patrols in and near the mouth of the bay. Despite the optimistic prediction made by Mervine in late 1861 that "garrisoned forts at these three harbors [Charlotte Harbor, Tampa Bay and Cedar Keys] would probably enable the United States to retain jurisdiction over this territory, if it is desirable. One or more gunboats plying up and down the coast, with the occasional call of supply vessels, would amply suffice to maintain a blockade," such was not the case. The bay was simply too wide and had too many small bays and inlets to prevent runners from escaping the port and returning on a regular basis.

In March 1862, Flag Officer William W. McKean, who had assumed command of the newly designated Eastern Gulf Blockading Squadron, reported to Secretary Welles that the captain of the USS *Ethan Allen*, on station at Tampa Bay, had sent a boat expedition from his ship to nearby Clearwater Harbor, which resulted in the capture of the schooner *Spitfire* and the sloops *Atlanta* and *Caroline*.

The same day, Welles sent a note to McKean and Flag Officer David G. Farragut, the commander of the Western Blockading Squadron, voicing optimism that "the Gulf Squadron having recently been so much enlarged and divided, the Department trusts that in future it may have no occasion to refer to the fact of vessels having run the blockade or to urge greater vigilance and the importance of cutting off communication with the rebel ports." Welles's optimism was misplaced, and blockade running continued even with the enlarged Union fleets. McKean, as field commanders are wont to do, immediately responded, "I can only say that no exertion has been wanting on my part to make the blockade as effective as possible with the force at my disposal, but I have never had a sufficient force of suitable vessels—sailing vessels being of little value to blockade steamers, especially when their draft of water is such as to prevent their lying close in, and in places where the current runs at the rate of three or four knots an hour."

There was an added responsibility faced by the blockaders operating along Florida's Gulf Coast. Although the coast was sparsely populated (only 8,567 inhabitants in the five counties that made up the Gulf shoreline), not all the inhabitants were supporters of the Confederate cause, and early on, the Union ships had to deal with refugees. In March 1862, McKean reported to Secretary of the Navy Welles that "several Union men residing in that vicinity have come off and claimed the protection of the Government, having been driven from their homes and families by the rebels." A month later, he reported:

> *The commander of the* Ethan Allen, *at Tampa Bay, has now upward of 25 men, women, and children* [who have been driven from their homes] *under the protection of his guns upon Egmont Key, and has been obliged to ration them from his ship to prevent starvation. The officers and crew of this ship, the* Kensington, *and other vessels in the harbor have taken up a subscription for their benefit, and I shall dispatch a vessel in a day or two with supplies for their relief, as I understand that the women and children are in a very suffering condition, not only from want of proper food, but clothing.*

The Union navy was poorly equipped to care for refugees, although it established camps on Egmont Key and Seahorse Key (near Cedar Keys) for them. This was a problem that would grow worse as the war went on and as Confederate fortunes worsened. Refugees provided valuable intelligence for blockaders and proved to be fertile recruiting ground for pilots and crews for Union ships. Henry A. Crane, the scourge of blockade runners on the Indian River, was a refugee from Tampa. As the Federal army began to conduct land raids, the pool of refugees again proved to be a source of manpower.

Despite the pervasive presence of Union ships off the coast of Tampa Bay, Confederate runners, usually laden with cotton and turpentine, continued to use the bay for making runs through the blockade, although Lieutenant J.C. Howell, captain of the USS *Tahoma*, reported on September 2, 1862, that "no vessel has attempted to run the blockade" at Tampa. Howell's report followed an earlier attempt by the Union navy to force the surrender of the town on April 13, when the USS *Beauregard*, a small bark, entered the main channel in Tampa Bay and proceeded to within one and a half miles of the town. The commander of the *Beauregard*, Acting Volunteer Lieutenant William B. Eaton, sent a boat ashore demanding that Confederate major R.B. Thomas, who commanded local Rebel forces, agree to "the unconditional surrender of the town of Tampa, Fla., together with all munitions of war and ordnance stores contained therein." When Thomas refused the surrender demand even after Eaton threatened, "If these terms are not complied with I will give you twenty-four hours to remove all women and children to a proper distance and then proceed to bombard the town," the *Beauregard* withdrew from the bay.

Confederate batteries were located along the banks of Tampa's main channel, and soldiers were stationed at various points to keep track of the blockading fleet. On the day before the *Beauregard* approached Tampa, a detachment from the ship was sent to Piney Point (near present-day Palmetto) to "shell out a company of soldiers who were stationed there to watch our movements and signal to the town. A few shells drove them away and a force was landed, and the barracks, consisting of log huts, destroyed."

There were many ships that used Tampa Bay and the surrounding inlets to hide from Union blockaders, to unload illicit cargoes or to begin their outward journey through the cordon of Federal vessels. On January 8, 1863, the USS *Tahoma* reported the capture of the "rebel sloop *Silas Henry*" loaded with sea-island cotton. On April 16, the USS *Hendrick Hudson* captured the schooner *Teresa* outside the bay near Egmont Key. A day later, the blockader *Wanderer* seized the schooner *Annie B.* with a cargo of seventeen bales of cotton. On May 5, the *Tahoma* captured the *Crazy Jane* with a cargo of turpentine and cotton. On June 6, the *Tahoma* took control of the schooner *Statesman*, loaded with cotton and within range of the protective Confederate guns at Gadsden's Point. On June 18, the *Tahoma* scored twice, seizing the English schooner *Harriet* on its way into Tampa Bay and, later that day, the English schooner *Mary Jane*, which had been beached inside Clearwater Harbor.

On October 13, the *Tahoma*, accompanied by the *Adela*, landed a party of one hundred men at Ballast Point with instructions to destroy the blockade runners *Scottish Chief* and *Kate Dale* owned by Captain James McKay Sr., which were located about five miles up the Hillsboro River and were loaded with cotton. The *Tahoma* and *Adela* engaged the Confederate shore batteries with their Parrott guns and "placed some stakes to the northward and eastward, as if intending to land there." The troops on shore responded to this perceived threat by sending a force to meet the expected invasion. The two Union ships withdrew and, later that night, under the cover of darkness, sent a landing party toward the runners. Former Tampa residents Henry A. Crane and J.A. Thompson guided the landing party toward the two target ships, which were burned.

Although the landing party was successful in burning the *Scottish Chief* and the *Kate Dale*, the raid was costly for the raiders. Three Union sailors were killed, eleven were wounded and four were captured by the Confederates.

Seven prisoners were captured by the landing force and brought back to the ships. The expedition was judged a success by the captain of the *Tahoma*, who noted the two blockade runners "destroyed were of light draft, not over 4 feet, and would have probably eluded me [as they ran the blockade]."

Admiral Bailey concurred in the captain's judgment and sent him a letter of commendation, in which he proclaimed, "The lesson taught to the rebels by this expedition, that their movements can be watched and thwarted by the daring of our seamen, even when carried on at a distance of several miles up a river whose mouth is protected by a fortified town, is of no small importance, and is calculated to depress them in proportion to the audacity and discipline displayed by our men."

The *Kate Dale* was rebuilt and resumed blockade running. On March 28, 1864, the captain of the USS *Sunflower* reported to Admiral Bailey, "I have the honor to report the capture of the sloop *Josephine* (formerly the *Kate Dale*), with 7 bales of cotton (6 sea island and 1 upland), from Tampa, bound to Havana, in Sarasota Sound, on the 24th instant."

The movement of ships in and out of Tampa Bay continued to nettle the commanders of the Union ships blockading the entrance to the harbor. On May 4, 1864, the USS *Sunflower* notified Admiral Bailey that it had captured the sloop *Neptune*, which had left Tampa Bay with a quantity of cotton estimated at about fifty-five bales. The *Sunflower* was part of a larger force of ships that, in cooperation with the Union army, landed at Tampa on May 5 and occupied the old Seminole Indian War Fort Brooke, which served as the headquarters of Confederate forces in the area as well as the town of Tampa itself. After capturing forty Confederates, but not finding further justification to stay, they threw most of the fort's armaments into the Hillsboro River, confiscated most of the city's food and supplies and left after just three days. Even this action did not put an end to blockade running from Tampa Bay, and small ships continued to make their way into and out of the bay.

One of the most unlikely, but busiest, ports for blockade runners was Bayport. Located at the mouth of the Weeki Wachee River, the port was ideal for the small, flat-bottomed coastal vessels that moved the produce of inland plantations to Cuba and brought back cargoes of salt, coffee, leather goods and liquors. Between Bayport and Cedar Keys, several small rivers—the Chassahowitzka River, the Pithlachascotee River, the Withlacoochee River and the Waccasassa River—provided sanctuary for small sloops, schooners and barks that collected outgoing cargo from the surrounding countryside. With small loads, perhaps as little as mere pounds of cotton and partial barrels of turpentine, these boats would make their way south to Bayport,

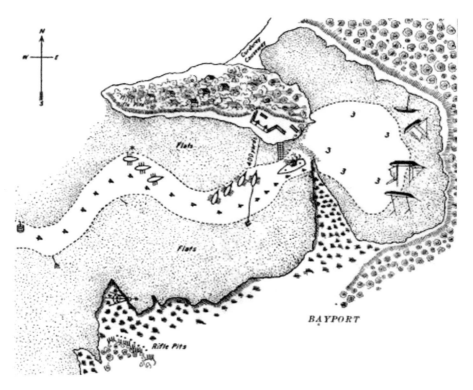

Bayport, a small port north of Tampa in Hernando County, was a favorite destination of blockade runners until the spring of 1863, when the port was raided by Union gunboats. *From* Official Records of the Union and Confederate Navies in the War of the Rebellion.

where several small cargoes would be consolidated for shipment to Havana by larger sailing vessels or steamers. The records of the East Gulf Blockading Squadron contain numerous reports of captures of these small runners, many of them unseaworthy but acceptable for close-in coastal journeys.

Although Bayport was considered to be a second-rate port, three Union boats, led by the USS *Sagamore*, arrived at the entrance to Bayport on April 3, 1863. The USS *St. Lawrence* and the USS *Fort Henry* completed the Union fleet. Immediately, boats from the *Sagamore* set out for a sloop lying inshore and quickly took possession of the vessel. It was the *Helen* out of Crystal River, carrying a cargo of corn. The crew from the *Sagamore* set it afire. Because of the shallow channel that led into the harbor, the *Sagamore* was forced to stay outside the harbor and sent its small boats, along with boats from the *St. Lawrence*, equipped with howitzers, to accompany the USS *Fort Henry*, which could navigate the channel. It took the *Fort Henry* two hours to move from the bay's entrance into the harbor.

The USS *Fort Henry* was part of the Union fleet that attacked Bayport on April 3, 1863. Although this attack failed to completely close down the port, it did destroy several blockade runners and more than three hundred bales of cotton. *Courtesy of the U.S. Naval Historical Center.*

As the Union ships proceeded into the harbor, they found five other vessels, the largest of which was a large schooner loaded with three hundred bales of cotton. Two small schooners and two sloops were observed in a bayou inside the harbor, grounded under the shelter of a thick stand of trees. As the *Fort Henry* and the boats from the *Sagamore* got closer to the schooner, which the Union sailors were determined to capture or destroy, they encountered heavy fire from two Confederate cannons in a battery protecting the channel. In addition, small arms fire from Confederate soldiers hidden along the banks of the channel made it difficult going for the raiding party. For fifteen minutes, Union sailors and Confederate soldiers fought an artillery duel that ended only when a shell from the howitzer onboard the *Sagamore*'s launch exploded over the Confederate battery, forcing the Rebel cannoneers to abandon their guns. The Union howitzers were also silenced when they broke their harnesses due to the recoil each time they fired. The small arms fire continued between the soldiers on shore and the raiders.

While the fighting was continuing, Confederate soldiers made their way to the cotton schooner and set it afire to prevent its capture by the Union forces. In addition, cotton stored in a nearby warehouse was set afire. Seeing that the fires set by the Confederates were "ignited to such an extent that rendered extinguishing impossible" and fearing that the ebb tide might leave his ship grounded in the harbor, Acting Lieutenant E.Y. McCauley, the captain of the *Fort Henry*, gave the order to withdraw. The raid was over.

The actions by Union ships at Bayport, while important, did not staunch the movement of blockade runners into and out of the port. The lack of a permanent blockading force at the mouth of the bay allowed runners to resume their activities almost immediately after the raid. On May 16, 1863, the Union schooner *Two Sisters* surprised the schooner *Oliver S. Breese* off Anclote Key. The *Breese* carried a general cargo from Havana and was bound for Bayport. The *Two Sisters* reported its launches had chased a blockade runner operating near the entrance to Bayport on the evening of October 4, but because darkness was falling we "lost sight of her in the darkness and she escaped." On October 15, 1863, the USS *Fox* reported the capture of the British steamer *Mail*, which had sailed from Bayport with a cargo of cotton.

Admiral Theodorus Bailey, responding to reports of activities continuing at Bayport, offered Lieutenant Commander A.A. Semmes, the commander of the blockading ships at Tampa, a strategy to deal with ships entering and departing Bayport. On December 8, 1863, he wrote to Semmes:

> *I understand that the channels in and out of Bayport and the rivers on your station, where the rebels are in the habit of running the blockade, are buoyed, or staked out. I wish, where you find that to be the case, that you will send boats and pilots in the night and change the position of those stakes, buoys, or marks in such new location as will infallibly plump their vessels on shore. The pilots should at the same time be ordered to observe carefully the situation of the channel from which they remove the marks, so that our own vessels may not get into the trap set for our enemies.*
>
> *After carrying out this order, watch carefully the nets thus set and pounce upon your prey when aground.*

Whether or not Semmes carried out the order was not included in the *Official Records of the Union Navy*. One thing is for certain: Bayport continued to function as a port for blockade runners. On July 3, 1864, the USS *Merrimac* reported the capture of the sloop *Henrietta* bound for Havana with a cargo of sixteen bales of cotton. The *Henrietta* had started its journey in Bayport.

Just a few days later, the USS *Magnolia* patrolling off the Bahama Islands reported the capture of three small boats loaded with nine bales of cotton and eight barrels of turpentine and headed for Nassau. The commander of the *Magnolia* reported the boats had left Bayport and "had been forty-two days on the passage, nine of which they had been in the Gulf, were almost destitute of provisions and water. There were two men in each boat, making six in all; the boats had neither name nor papers."

In July 1864, the Union army, under the command of Brigadier General Daniel P. Woodbury, decided to conduct a raid on the small village of Brooksville in Hernando County. Brooksville was a center for the collection of cattle for the Confederate government, and the cattle collected there were shipped to Lee's army in Virginia and the Army of Tennessee. Both Rebel armies were dependent on Florida cattle for sustenance, and Woodbury sought to deprive them of this valuable source of fresh meat. As Union soldiers approached Brooksville, a second column of Federal troops was sent toward Bayport.

Arriving in Bayport, the Yankee troops found the village abandoned by Confederate soldiers. Supported by gunboats *Ariel* and *Seabird* that arrived in the port unopposed, the troops collected some 140 bales of cotton that were awaiting shipment out of the port. Although some 40 bales of loose cotton were accidentally destroyed by fire, the remainder was loaded aboard the *Ariel*. After remaining in the village for a single night, the Union forces left the next day. Before leaving, James J. Russell, acting master of the *Ariel*, set fire to the building used as the customs house and all the boats, scows and cotton storage houses in the village. With Bayport burning, the three schooners left and returned to the army's headquarters in Fort Meyers.

Even this temporary occupation by Federal forces did not end the use of Bayport for running the blockade, however. In February 1865, a force of Union soldiers from Cedar Keys, under the command of Major Edmund C. Weeks, carried out another raid on the small port. The results of this raid were not reported.

On February 17, 1865, the USS *Mahaska* reported the capture of the schooner *Delia* off the entrance of Bayport, the last blockade runner trying to use the port. Lieutenant Commander William Gibson, the captain of the *Mahaska*, described the *Delia* as "a center-board schooner of apparently about 80 tons burden. Her cargo consists of pig lead and some cases of sabers. Part of her cargo was thrown overboard. I have taken some 15 gallons of rum belonging to her on board this ship for safe-keeping."

At long last, Bayport's role in running the Union blockade played out.

Chapter 9

The Blockade

From Cedar Keys to Pensacola

In fact the blockade of St. Marks, Apalachicola, and Pensacola is the blockade of this coast. A single gunboat for each of the two first-named ports would suffice…The narrow, crooked, and shoal passage to St. Marks might be easily obstructed by sinking a vessel in it…Apalachicola might be converted into a cotton port if desired; the excellently sheltered bay of St. Vincent affording a fine roadstead for a fleet.
—Captain S.F. Du Pont, commanding, Blockade Strategy Board, September 3, 1861

Although Flag Officer William Mervine, the first commander of the newly formed Gulf Blockading Squadron, had only fifteen ships to blockade all the ports along the Gulf from Key West at the tip of Florida to Brownsville at the mouth of the Rio Grande in Texas, Union naval authorities thought that this limited number would be sufficient to do the job. Of these fifteen ships, only four were stationed along the Gulf Coast of the Sunshine State. Although the subdivision of the Gulf Blockading Squadron into the East Gulf and West Gulf Blockading Squadrons in February 1862 and the addition of newly purchased ships to the fleets alleviated the problem somewhat, the Union blockade was still stretched thin.

In the survey made by the navy in September 1861, Captain Samuel Francis Du Pont (he was the only member of the wealthy du Pont family to capitalize the first letter of his last name) and the other members of the Strategy Board, which was charged with developing an overall strategy to make the blockade effective, recommended that the area between Pensacola and Cedar Keys be considered a single patrol area. This 290-mile stretch

Above: Confiscated by the United States in Key West harbor on April 12, 1861, the *Wanderer* was a former slave ship that served as a mail carrier, coal tender and water ship for other vessels in the East Gulf Blockading Squadron. *Courtesy of the U.S. Naval Historical Center.*

Left: David Levy Yulee was an antebellum United States senator from Florida, a large planter and a prewar entrepreneur. In 1860, he opened the Florida Railroad, which ran from Fernandina on the east coast to Cedar Keys. Within a few months of opening, the road was closed when both Fernandina and Cedar Key were attacked by Union forces. The road continued to operate during the war in short stretches, but many miles of its tracks were taken up and used to build other railroads. *Courtesy of the Florida State Photographic Archives.*

of coast abutted the most heavily populated areas of the Sunshine State and was in proximity to the major plantation counties in Florida. During the late antebellum period, Apalachicola and St. Marks had been the major entrepôts for cotton and tobacco shipped to Europe and Northern states and for luxury items coming into the state. A short 22-mile railroad connected St. Marks with the state capital, Tallahassee. To the south, the deep harbor of Cedar Keys became important in 1860 when David Levy Yulee selected it as the western terminus for his Florida Railroad. Along the coast between Cedar Keys and Pensacola were numerous small rivers and bays that could be used for blockade running activities—the Aucilla (Ocilla), the Suwannee, the Steinhatchee, the Ochlockonee and the Apalachicola Rivers and the bays at St. Andrews and Cape San Blas.

The harbor at Pensacola was quickly eliminated as a blockade running port because the guns at Fort Pickens ranged the harbor and any ship venturing in or out was subject to intense cannon fire. Outside the harbor, Union ships maintained a constant guard. In May 1862, General Sam Jones ordered all Confederate troops out of the city and, after destroying boats, naval facilities and sawmills, abandoned the town to Union forces. Pensacola was firmly in the hands of Federal troops for the remainder of the war.

Cedar Keys—which encompassed the town of Cedar Key (Way Key), Atsena Otie (Depot) Key, Seahorse Key, Salt Key and a number of smaller islands—was a primary concern for the blockading squadron since it was the western end of the Florida Railroad, which stretched across the Florida peninsula to Fernandina. The deep channels and railroad attracted blockade runners during 1861 because it was easy to enter and depart the port from a number of channels. The ready access to the inland cotton plantations, turpentine stills and sawmills by way of the railroad made accumulating outbound cargoes easy, while the same railroad provided a quick and easy way to move contraband into the interior of the state. In October 1861, Flag Officer William W. McKean, the commander of the then Gulf Blockading Squadron, informed Union secretary of the navy Gideon Welles that he was assigning a single steamer to blockade the port. The presence of a solitary blockader off the coast of Cedar Keys did little to deter the use of the port by Southern ships.

On January 6, 1862, Flag Officer Samuel F. Du Pont sent an urgent message to the captain of the USS *Florida* from his flagship USS *Wabash* in Port Royal, South Carolina, directing the *Florida* to Cedar Keys "to intercept the *Gladiator*, heavily loaded with arms and munitions, or her cargo transshipped into small vessels and forwarded from Nassau, where the *Gladiator* had arrived from England…The close blockade of this [Atlantic] coast now, and the prevalence of easterly gales has, I am induced to believe, directed the vessels running the blockade to Cedar Keys, from which they are sent up by Florida Railroad to Savannah." Du Pont, aware that he had dispatched one of his ships into the Gulf, which was under the operational command of Flag Officer William W. McKean, pointedly instructed the *Florida*'s captain, "I do not mean that you shall assume the blockade of Cedar Keys, but only to watch for a time for the *Gladiator*."

The day before Du Pont sent the *Florida* toward Cedar Keys, McKean had issued instructions to Commander G.F. Emmons of the USS *Hatteras* "to proceed to Cedar Keys and endeavor to capture or destroy a small armed steamer and schooner said to be at that place." Although Du Pont dispatched the *Florida* because he could not reach McKean in time to stop the *Gladiator*, this breach of command authority engendered a feud between the two commanders.

The *Hatteras* arrived at Cedar Keys on January 7 and immediately landed a force of sailors and marines who attacked the railhead of the Florida Railroad on Way Key. Despite a vigorous defense by a company of cavalry and local civilians, the raiders managed to destroy buildings, engines and a considerable length of tracks before retreating to their ship. That did not end the raid, however, and the *Hatteras* then sank or burned seven blockade runners in the harbor at Depot Key before sending a raiding party ashore to destroy the harbor facilities. The men of the *Hatteras* also destroyed a Confederate battery of two thirty-two-pounders on Seahorse Key. The ship then departed the area.

On January 28, McKean dispatched the gunboat USS *Tahoma* to the Cedar Keys area with orders to enforce "a rigid blockade of that place and also to prevent the reoccupation of Seahorse Key by the rebel forces." The captain of the *Tahoma* was also ordered to confiscate the lumber that was stored on Seahorse Key and protect it, as "in the event of occupying the position with a military force it would be useful in the erection of barracks."

Two months later, on March 6, Cedar Keys was visited by the *James L. Davis*, which reported that Depot Key and Seahorse Key had been evacuated by Confederate forces but that Way Key had more than one thousand Southern troops, which "if they had a rifle cannon they could very easy riddle this ship, as I am in a position where I can not get out over the bar except at high water and a fair wind." Fortunately, the Confederates on Way Key had no rifled cannon, and the *James L. Davis* was able to depart soon afterward and resume its patrol along the coast. On March 10, the captain of the *Davis* reported the capture of a schooner, the *Florida*, which was "bound to some port on the Florida coast between Apalachicola and Cedar Keys" with a cargo of "250 bags of coffee, soda ash, soap, spool cotton, hoop skirts, and dry goods assorted" worth about $15,000.

In 1864, the Union army occupied Cedar Keys, and Colonel Benjamin R. Townsend of the Second U.S. Colored Infantry used Way Key as his headquarters. A Union prisoner of war camp was built on Seahorse Key, while a separate camp on the island was home to hundreds of refugees and Union sympathizers from north Florida. The Union navy built and maintained a supply facility on Depot Key. From Cedar Keys, the Union army launched raids into the interior of Florida, although with limited success. The continued presence of Union troops at Cedar Keys ended its usefulness as a port for blockade runners.

The Union blockaders controlled both Pensacola and Cedar Keys, but despite their best efforts, they were never completely successful in stopping runners from using St. Andrews Bay, the Suwannee River and Apalachee Bay. Stephen Russell Mallory, a former United States senator from Florida, served as the Confederate secretary of the navy and tried to get the Southern naval forces organized and equipped. Despite his best efforts, Mallory was not successful in putting together a fleet that could lift the Union blockade. Still, he was hopeful that ways could be found to circumvent it.

In support of the Confederate diplomatic attempt to use cotton to force European nations to recognize the newly formed Southern government, Governor John Milton of Florida issued orders to Colonel R.F. Floyd on November 25, 1861, to prevent blockade runners from leaving Apalachicola with cargoes of cotton. Milton's instructions were specific: "Permit no vessel with cotton, to leave Apalachicola; issue an order prohibiting it; if attempted, sink the vessel. Arrest and place in close confinement any and every individual who shall attempt to ship cotton from Apalachicola. With regard to other descriptions of cargo, exercise a sound discretion." Floyd put Milton's prohibition into effect immediately and, on November 27, reported, "Your orders respecting cotton shall be strictly observed. Turpentine is also forbidden to be sent abroad. I learned that 300 bales of cotton had lately arrived here for shipment. I will order it back to the river at once." Somewhat confused about the cotton embargo, Milton sent a telegram to Mallory on November 29 requesting clarification: "Shall vessels be permitted to go from Apalachicola, risking the blockade, with turpentine, to procure acids for telegraphic operations, coffee, etc., from Havana? Vessels ready and stopped by my order. Answer immediately." Mallory replied that he saw no reason why ships loaded with such cargoes should not be allowed to exit the port.

Apalachicola, the port at the mouth of Apalachicola River, was raided often and early by sailors from Union gunboats. In early 1862, Florida's governor, John Milton, ordered Confederate installations in the area around the town abandoned and the approximately 650 Southern soldiers who had manned them transferred to Fernandina in anticipation of a Federal attack there. On March 25, 1862, H.S. Stellwagen, the commander of the USS *Meredita*, reported to Flag Officer William W. McKean that "not a soldier, cannon, or apparently any weapon of war remains." Of the 600 persons— "about a dozen white families, a few slaves, and some Spanish fishermen"— who remained in the town, Stellwagen reported that many of them were strong Unionists but did not want to make a public stand of being so because "threats have often been made to hang or to starve them as damn Yankees, traitors to the South." Confederate sympathizers made "threats…to burn the whole town if they hold intercourse with us."

General John Newton, who replaced General Daniel P. Woodbury as the Union army commander in southern Florida, pursued an aggressive policy of joint army-navy raids along the coast. He tried to capture Tallahassee by striking through St. Marks but was stopped at the Battle of Natural Bridge. Tallahassee remained the only Confederate state capital east of the Mississippi to escape capture by Union forces. *Courtesy of the Library of Congress.*

For the next three years, Union gunboats made regular visits to Apalachicola, and some Union military officers wanted to occupy the town. As late as August 1864, Major General William Tecumseh Sherman, on the outskirts of Atlanta, urged Major General H.W. Halleck, the chief of staff of the Federal army, to persuade Admiral Farragut "to send a few of his vessels to demolish old Fort St. Marks and then go up the Apalachicola as far as the depth of water will permit. The old arsenal at the mouth of Flint River is an important post, to be destroyed or even threatened."

Although naval raids continued around both St. Marks and Apalachicola, it was not until March 1865 that Union general John Newton launched a major raid through St. Marks toward Tallahassee. Even that was a disaster, as Newton's forces were beaten back by a hastily assembled group of Confederate regulars, military cadets and civilians at Natural Bridge. The Union army beat a hasty retreat back to St. Marks.

The Union navy did have success against blockade runners operating in the waters around Apalachicola and St. Marks. On February 5, 1862, the USS *Marion* gave a detailed report of blockade runners in the area. The schooner *Phoenix*, with a cargo of between 500 and 600 bales of cotton, was at Apalachicola waiting to run the blockade. The schooner *Kate L. Bruce*, which ran the blockade into Apalachicola the previous summer, was still there, laden with a cargo of fruit. The schooner *William P. Benson* was at St. Andrews after running the blockade two weeks earlier with a cargo of coffee from Havana. It was loading a cargo of about 150 bales of cotton for the voyage back.

In April 1862, the sloop *Octavia*, pilot boats *Cygnet* and *Mary Olivia* and schooners *New Island*, *Floyd* and *Rose* were captured at Apalachicola by men from the USS *Meredita*. The *Rose* was loaded with a full cargo of cotton. On October 16, 1862, under small arms fire from an unknown source, men from the USS *Fort Henry* recovered a sloop, the *G.L. Brockenborough*, which had been scuttled with sixty-four bales of cotton on board. Two months later, the USS *Roebuck* seized the British schooner *Kate*, which attempted to run the blockade at St. Marks with a cargo of salt, copper, coffee and liquors. The USS *Port Royal* reported on April 24, 1863, that an armed party from the ship had landed at Apalachicola and found twelve bales of cotton and an assortment of munitions—twenty-five canister, thirty chain and fourteen oblong bar iron shot, all for thirty-two-pounder guns. A month later, on May 25, the *Port Royal* captured the sloop *Fashion* with a cargo of fifty bales of sea-island cotton.

Despite the diligence of Union blockaders and even the hostility of many in Apalachicola, the stretch of territory between Pensacola and Cedar Keys continued to be a hotbed of blockade running throughout the war. Even the Confederate government encouraged the use of the myriad inlets, bays and rivers as ports of ingress and egress for the illicit cargoes of Southern ships.

Realizing that the primary and secondary ports of the Confederacy were closed to commerce, Confederate secretary of the navy Stephen Mallory sought to negate the blockade by using the small inlets and rivers between Cedar Keys and Pensacola to bring in critically needed supplies. He penned a letter to Commander James D. Bulloch, the Confederate purchase agent in Great Britain, on March 29, 1864, requesting him to purchase two or more steamers expressly for the trade between Cuba or the Bahamas and certain points in Florida, "say St. Marks, Apalachicola, the Swannee [*sic*] River and St. Andrew's

Bay." The ships he wanted were very specific to running the blockade, and he cautioned Bulloch that "their draft of water should not exceed, with everything on board, four feet. This, I am aware, is very small draft for a seagoing vessel, but the shallow waters of the Florida inlets demand it."

On June 24, 1864, he pointed out the Florida ports of Apalachicola and St. Marks as possible targets for quick raids by the Confederate cruiser *Florida*, under the command of Lieutenant Charles Manigault Morris. These ports, he noted, were "each blockaded by one steamer (a side-wheel), and should you deem it advisable you might perhaps capture them, send them into St. Mark's under prize crews, and leave the Gulf at once." Morris did not accept these directions and instead sailed east to Tenerife in the Canaries and from there to Bahia, Brazil, arriving on October 4, 1864. While in the Brazilian port, the *Florida* was attacked by the USS *Wachusett* on the night of October 7 while its captain was ashore with half his crew. The hapless *Florida* was then towed out to sea and taken as a prize to the United States. This illegal attack was protested by Brazil as a violation of its sovereignty, but its protests came to naught.

As late as February 1865, Mallory remained hopeful that ships could be found that could evade the blockaders and find sanctuary along the northern coast of Florida. On February 24, he instructed Commander John N. Maffitt of the Confederate navy to sell the CSS *Owl* and the CSS *Chameleon* in Nassau and use the money from the sale to purchase "well built and fast steamers, drawing under 6 feet when fully laden." Mallory's order stressed "the urgent importance of getting in our supplies, and particularly small arms…into St. Marks, or any other port accessible to us in Florida, or any where this side of the Mississippi." Lest he tie Maffitt's hands too much, Mallory concluded, "You are familiar with the Gulf coast of Florida, and you will recognize by a glance at the charts several places between Apalachicola and Tampa Bay at which they might enter."

Mallory's belief that Confederate fortunes might somehow be sustained by the use of small steamers putting into remote inlets and bays was nothing more than a desperate hope, but he was out of touch with the realities on the ground. Apalachicola had no defenses against Union naval raids, nor did St. Marks, and following the occupation of Cedar Keys, the Union army made regular forays along the coast and into the interior of Florida. Events elsewhere had simply made blockade running on Florida coasts irrelevant by late 1864.

David Coles, in an article in the *Florida Historical Quarterly* in 1992, reported that in three and a half years, the 85-ship fleet of blockading squadrons captured or destroyed 283 Confederate blockade runners.

Chapter 10
Contrabands and Kettles

U.S. Flagship St. Lawrence
Key West, April 21, 1863

On the 27th ultimo, as the bark Pursuit *was lying off Gadsden's Point in Tampa Bay, on blockade, a smoke was discovered on the beach, and shortly afterwards three persons made their appearance, waving a white flag. Acting Volunteer Lieutenant Randall, in command of the* Pursuit, *supposing them to be escaped contrabands or others, wishing to communicate with the vessel, sent a boat in, in charge of Acting Master H.K. Lapham, with a flag of truce flying. On the boat nearing the beach, two of the parties were seen to be clothed in female apparel, with their hands and faces blackened, and one of them appeared to be overcome with joy, exclaiming, "Thank God! Thank God! I am free." On the boat touching the beach, the female dresses were thrown off, and it then became evident that they were white men, disguised for the purpose of decoying the boat on shore. Immediately afterwards about 100 armed men arose from the bushes around about and demanded the surrender of the boat, which being refused, they fired a volley of musketry into her, wounding the officer in charge and three of the crew. The fire was returned by the boat's crew, some firing and the rest hauling the boat off until they were out of range. As soon as the firing commenced, the* Pursuit *was sprung and her battery brought to bear, and four shells fired amongst the rebels, but probably without effect.*

The gunboat Tahoma, *arriving at Tampa Bay the next day, her commander having been informed of the treacherous conduct of the rebels, ordered the* Pursuit *down the bay, and proceeded with the U.S. schooner* Beauregard *up to bombard the town. It blowing a norther at the time, it was impossible to do anything more than to try the range of the*

Beauregard's rifle, which was done with satisfactory results. On the 2d instant, the commander of the Tahoma, *while returning to his vessel from a closer inspection of the battery, had three shots fired at him. The* Beauregard *was then sent as near the battery as was possible, and both vessels commenced firing on the town, hitting some of the houses, but what other damage was done could not be ascertained. I herewith enclose the acting assistant surgeon's report of the wounded on board the bark* Pursuit.
—Theodorus Bailey, acting rear admiral, commanding East Gulf Blockading Squadron

The Union blockade was not entirely focused on capturing or sinking blockade runners. Captains of Federal ships sought to inflict as much economic damage as possible on Confederate states by actively encouraging slaves to flee their owners and take shelter on Union ships. By the summer of 1861, "contrabands" were employed by the United States Navy at the rate of ten dollars a month, plus one ration of food per day. Usually restricted to performing the most menial tasks aboard ship—seaman, ordinary seaman, fireman or coal bearer—contrabands were essential because of the rapid buildup of the navy and because of the paucity of available white recruits. Contrabands were also useful sources of intelligence about Confederate military activities in a particular area and the navigability of the creeks,

Runaway slaves or "contrabands" were a valuable source of intelligence for Union forces in Florida. In addition, many joined the Federal army and navy. *Courtesy of the Florida Photographic Archives.*

bays and rivers that were so numerous along the Southern coasts. Some contrabands performed yeoman service as pilots for Union vessels.

Florida was particularly vulnerable to this kind of economic warfare. In 1860, the population of the Sunshine State was about 145,000 persons. Of this number, fully half were slaves, primarily employed in the cultivation of cotton and tobacco before the war and located in the northern half of the state. With 15,000 white Floridians engaged in some kind of military service, the number of whites controlling the state's slave population was reduced to perhaps 60,000, including women and children.

When the war came in 1861, a large number of slaves was transferred from the plantations and farms and set to making salt in large, sprawling complexes located on the coasts of the Florida peninsula. Salt, which was much more valuable than cotton or tobacco, was used in preserving food, tanning leather for shoes and manufacturing gunpowder. It was such a scarce and critically needed item—one estimate was that twenty thousand bushels were required daily in the Confederacy—that some Southern states established state-owned works along the Florida coasts to satisfy the needs of their citizens.

At first, the Union had no fixed policy regarding the treatment of contrabands who made their way to Federal forces. Yet from the very beginning of the war, runaway slaves and free persons of color sought shelter with Union land and naval forces. Providing a safe haven for these individuals created a dilemma for the United States because the Federal government did not want to antagonize the slave states that were allied with it, but at the same time, leaders recognized the fact that slaves were used frequently to strengthen the military of the Confederacy. Slaves were used as labor to build fortifications, as mule skinners and wagon drivers, as horse wranglers, as cooks or as general labor for the myriad tasks involved with the movement or supplying of an army. Slaves often accompanied their Southern masters when they reported for duty.

While some slave owners made their slaves available *gratis*, the Confederate central government and various state governments quickly became contractors for slave labor, usually at the rate of twenty-five dollars a month. The use of slave labor by the Confederate military freed thousands of white men for active duty in frontline units, which greatly enhanced the limited resources of the South. Not only did slaves play a vital role in the day-to-day operations of the Confederate military, but their larger importance was due to their continued presence on the farms and plantations of the South, producing foodstuffs and cotton.

Slaves performed many tasks in Confederate Florida during the Civil War. They worked as laborers on plantations, skilled fishermen, salt workers and draymen. This drawing of antebellum Tallahassee depicts slaves performing a number of tasks. *Courtesy of the Florida Photographic Archives.*

Although Union officials were aware of the essential roles played by slaves in the Southern war effort, engrained racism and the legal definition of slaves as private property prevented them from encouraging the mass defection of the slave population. The increasingly large number of contrabands making their way to the Union army and navy, particularly in Virginia, during the first months of the war forced Secretary of the Navy Gideon Welles to slowly develop a policy to deal with them. In September 1861, an exchange of correspondence between him and his commanders detailed the evolution of this policy. On September 18, Welles ordered Captain Thomas T. Craven, the commander of the Potomac Flotilla, to "allow clothes to the contrabands who are engaged in any *public services* in your flotilla."

By September 25, Welles further expanded his orders to Craven by formulating a broad policy for the treatment of contrabands. He wrote:

> *The Department finds it necessary to adopt a regulation with respect to the large and increasing number of persons of color, commonly known as contraband, now subsisted at the navy yards and on board ships of war. They can neither be expelled from the service to which they have resorted,*

nor can they be maintained unemployed, and it is not proper that they should be compelled to render necessary and regular services without a stated compensation. You are therefore authorized, when their services can be made useful, to enlist them for the naval service, under the same forms and regulations as apply to other enlistments. They will be allowed, however, no higher rating than boys, at a compensation of $10 per month and one ration a day.

With a single order, Welles established a policy that would endure throughout the war. Long before African Americans were recruited for service in the Union army, the navy was making positive uses—although limited—of them. With minor changes, this policy would continue to dictate the role African Americans would play in the United States Navy until World War II.

Despite Welles's order to "to enlist them for the naval service" when their services could be useful, not all Union naval officers immediately embraced his policy decision. On November 8, just days after the policy had been proclaimed, Lieutenant A.D. Harrell of the USS *Union* wrote to Craven about twenty-three contrabands the ship *Island Belle* had picked up. "I think it would be a good stroke of policy to return these negroes [*sic*] to their owners," he wrote. "It would tend to put a stop to the wholesale desertion that is now going on, and relieve us of a most unpleasant difficulty."

Despite the reluctance of some officers to carry out the policy regarding contrabands, the Union navy slowly began to accept them on board ships and transferred them to collection points within Union lines. Lookout Point, Maryland, was one of the first camps for contrabands established by the navy, but as the navy expanded its operations along the entire 3,500 miles of Southern coasts, additional camps were built.

In Florida, contrabands who sought refuge with ships of the East Gulf Blockading Squadron were sent to Key West in the first years of the war. Later, camps for contrabands, Confederate deserters and white Unionist refugees were established at Fort Myers, Egmont Key and Seahorse Key. These camps became fertile recruiting grounds for the Federal army in the creation of the U.S. Second Florida Cavalry in mid-1863 as it sought to curtail the shipment of Florida cattle to Southern armies. At the same time, Union general Daniel P. Woodbury began recruiting African Americans from the camps for service in the Second Infantry Regiment, United States Colored Troops. Union army units were also recruited from white refugees and deserters in southwest Florida and in Pensacola, where Brigadier General Alexander Asboth received permission to create the First Florida Cavalry in December 1863.

Jacksonville, which was occupied and evacuated four times during the war by Union troops, also became the destination of contrabands fleeing northeast Florida. The contrabands who made their way to Union lines were collected by the army and transported to Fernandina and Port Royal. Once again, slaves became a valuable source of intelligence for the Union troops operating in that corner of the Sunshine State, and once again, contrabands were recruited for service in the Federal army.

The Emancipation Proclamation, which President Abraham Lincoln issued on January 1, 1863, gave additional impetus to the movement of slaves from their masters to Union lines. The proclamation not only guaranteed the liberty of contrabands who successfully arrived behind Union lines but also settled the question of how the military should treat them by allowing the enrollment of freed slaves into the United States military, a policy the Union navy had been following since late 1861. During the war, nearly 200,000 blacks, most of them former slaves, joined the Union army, which significantly expanded its size. The Confederacy, which excluded the use of African Americans in fighting roles until March 1865, lost out on this valuable source of additional manpower.

Not all slaves fled their masters on their own initiative. However, large numbers took advantage of the presence of blockading ships offshore to surrender to landing parties and ask for refuge. Because of the proximity

The Emancipation Proclamation, issued by Abraham Lincoln on January 1, 1863, changed the focus of the Civil War from a political conflict to a moral crusade. It also ended any chance at all of the Confederacy receiving diplomatic recognition from European nations. *Courtesy of the Library of Congress.*

to the coast of saltworks that employed hundreds of slaves, many of the contrabands gathered on the west coast of Florida took advantage of the flight of masters and Confederate troops when Union raiding parties arrived to leave their work. With each slave defection, salt production was reduced, and the reduction of the amount of salt available severely limited the ability of Southerners to preserve food or to ship meat to Confederate armies in the field.

Salt prices started to rise with the outbreak of war in 1861 and continued to do so until it ended in 1865. On February 5, 1862, the captain of the USS *Marion* reported that "small boxes of salt, about half a bushel, [are selling] at $5" in Apalachicola, which had multiple saltworks nearby. In Atlanta just a month later, a single sack of salt (roughly a bushel) cost $22 (Confederate), while the price rose to $35 per sack by mid-April. By mid-May, the price had risen to $40 a sack. By 1865, salt brought $50 (Confederate) per bushel. The demand for salt was so great that blockade runners included quantities of salt as part of their inbound cargoes. Manifest of captured blockade runners routinely included multiple sacks of the commodity, duly noted by Union ship crews, who shared in the money generated by the sale of the captured cargoes.

Operators of saltworks were exempted from Confederate military service and allowed to operate without government interference. Slaves were used to cut wood to fuel the large boilers that converted seawater into unrefined salt and for the hard manual labor required to move large quantities of salt water to the boilers. In addition, the packaging of crude salt and the transportation of the finished product to ports and villages required additional labor, much of which was provided by slaves.

Two aspects of salt production, particularly in Florida, played into the hands of Union forces. First, many of the saltworks were located within a few hundred feet of the Atlantic or the Gulf and were therefore vulnerable to raids by gunboats and launches from Union ships. Second, Union vessels very early in the war instituted a policy of accepting contrabands on board and transporting them to collection points where they would be housed and fed by naval authorities, and saltworks were often places where contrabands could be collected easily.

There were dangers, however, for the Union fleet as it made raids on saltworks. Sometimes, Confederate forces were assigned to protect such works, and Union raiders always ran the risk of being attacked by these units. On October 8, 1862, a combined expedition from the USS *Tahoma* and the USS *Somerset* attacked saltworks on the mainland near Seahorse Key but were able to carry out the job only after "twenty or thirty armed guerrillas were put to flight by the shell, shrapnel, and canister." The Union raid resulted in the destruction of sixty kettles, capable of producing 150 bushels of salt each day.

Between November 24 and December 8, 1862, Union ships attacked a number of saltworks located along the coast from Pensacola to St. Andrews Bay. Raids were carried out against many of these saltworks again in early 1863. As the blockade was strengthened with the addition of more ships, anti-saltworks raids were increased as the year went along. New raids targeted salt-making sites in Ocala Lake, Alligator Bay, St. Josephs Bay, St. Andrews Bay and Cedar Keys. Virtually every patrol of each Union ship included a raid on saltworks between 1863 and 1865. Raiding was dangerous business. On November 14, 1864, for example, the captain of the USS *Nita* reported that an expedition sent to destroy saltworks in the Tampa Bay area suffered one man wounded and five taken as prisoners by Confederate soldiers. The saltworks was described as quite extensive and belonging to the Confederate government.

Raiding saltworks was also frustrating for Union sailors. They expended considerable time and energy—always with the possibility of an armed attack hanging over them—breaking up saltworks that were almost always put back into operation within a few days. Simplicity was the key to operating saltworks. A few iron boilers, ladles and plenty of firewood were the basic requirements, although some used elaborate systems of settling vats, condensers, sheet-iron boilers and strainers. The smallest and simplest of these operations could produce five to twenty-five bushels of salt per day, while the more sophisticated works could produce five hundred bushels. The Lesley, Hope and Ryals Company, which operated twenty-five miles southwest of Brooksville, had elaborate brick furnaces manned by slaves but produced only ten to fifteen bushels of salt each day.

On October 26, 1862, the USS *Kingfisher* reported that the destruction of saltworks near St. Joseph's by that vessel had cost more than $20,000 to build. Acting Lieutenant Joseph P. Couthouy, who commanded the *Kingfisher*, reported that two refugees from Georgia who had been taken on board the ship described the raid as "a heavy blow to the rebels, and created great excitement throughout Georgia and Florida, these works having been the main source on which those States relied for a supply of salt for the winter's provisions for their troops, and that it was a greater injury to the rebels than if we had captured 20,000 prisoners."

Although the Union ships and crews continued their raids on saltworks along the coast, the industry expanded to such a point that several thousand men were employed in the industry and thousands of bushels were being manufactured each day and shipped to the interior of Florida. From there, much of the salt went north to Confederate armies and civilians in other states. Still, the blockading ships tried their best to bring about the complete destruction of salt making in Florida. One ship, the USS *Bloomer*, and its tender, *Caroline*, joined the bark *Restless* in operations against saltworks in Ocala Lake and St. Andrews Bay in December 1863. Between December 2 and December 28, the three vessels, acting alone or together, destroyed some 380 different saltworks in the area, capable of producing more than one thousand bushels a day.

On the first day of the raids, the *Restless* destroyed three large works in Lake Ocala, including six steamboat boilers cut in half lengthwise and eleven two-hundred-gallon kettles, capable of producing 130 bushels a day. Two large flatboats and six ox carts were demolished, while a large quantity of salt was thrown into the lake.

Next, the *Restless* moved to St. Andrews Bay, assisted by the *Bloomer* and the *Caroline*, which had arrived on December 10. A crew of three officers and forty-eight men from the *Restless* joined a seven-man crew from the newly arrived ships and moved into the West Bay area, "where the rebel Government's salt works were first destroyed, and which produced 400 bushels daily. At this place there were 27 buildings, 22 large boilers, and some 200 kettles, averaging 200 gallons each, all of which were destroyed, together with 5,000 bushels of salt, and some storehouses containing some three months' provisions—the whole estimated at half a million of dollars."

The expedition then proceeded "down the bay, destroying private salt works which lined each side for a distance of seven miles, to the number of 198 different establishments, averaging two boilers and two kettles each, together with a large quantity of salt; 507 kettles were dug up and rendered useless, and over 200 buildings were destroyed, together with 27 wagons and five large flatboats." In his report to Secretary of the Navy Gideon Welles, Admiral Theodorus Bailey placed the value of the destroyed property at $3 million.

In addition to the destruction of the saltworks, the raiding party took seventeen prisoners and brought thirty-one contrabands on board who were "employed at those works [and] gladly availed themselves of this opportunity to escape, and were of great service in pointing out the places where the kettles were buried for concealment." The *Restless* then proceeded to within one hundred yards of the town of St. Andrews, where Bailey had information that Confederate troops were hidden, and shelled it. By the third shell, the houses in the town had caught on fire, and thirty-two of them burned. Southern soldiers were observed fleeing the inferno and taking refuge in the surrounding woods.

Not all raids were on the scale of the St. Andrews raid. Most were conducted by a few men sent ashore in boats from Union ships to destroy the operations of small works consisting of two or three kettles. On June 7, 1864, the USS *Sunflower* reported a successful attack on saltworks belonging to a "Mr. Hooker" in Tampa Bay. The Hooker works were typical of private operations and consisted of four very large kettles and large furnaces. Hiding saltworks from the vigilant eyes of Union blockaders was not easy since the operations of such works depended on the use of large amounts of cut wood to heat the boilers. Often—as in the case of the unsuccessful attack on saltworks near Gadsden's Point in Tampa Bay by the USS *Nita* on November 12, 1864—the raid was launched after sailors observed plumes of smoke from heating fires spiraling into the sky to try and "ascertain the cause of many fires in the vicinity of Gadsden's Point and Old Tampa Bay." Any column of smoke observed along the largely unpopulated coasts of Florida merited closer examination by Union ships.

Raids against saltworks continued to the very end of the war. Lieutenant Commander William Gibson of the USS *Mahaska* reported the destruction of saltworks at St. Marks as late as March 21, 1865. "The salt works here are of vital importance to the rebels," he reported. "After our attack salt went from $30 to $50 per bushel, Confederate money."

Although Union ships blockading the coasts of Florida saw very little in the way of ship-to-ship combat, they performed valuable services in weakening the Confederate military and destroying Southern morale. Although some historians are skeptical about the efficacy of the blockade in stopping the majority of blockade runners into and out of Southern ports, there can be little doubt that the blockade proved efficient in depriving the Southern states of large amounts of critically needed material. "The high profile of the blockade in the minds of southerners and Europeans," wrote historian Joe Knetsch, "was worth a hundred Yankee regiments in the field. Psychologically the constant presence of Union ships off southern shores was visible proof that southern independence was unlikely."

Chapter 11
Fish, Corn and Citrus

We are ransacking every portion of the Confederacy, and, in addition, I have
authorized enterprises and contracts of even an extraordinary character to procure
supplies from abroad, even from the United States. I do not despair of these means
proving successful, but it is not to be disguised that painful uncertainty rests upon the
matter, and that the utmost prudence and economy in the use of the supplies we have
are exacted by our circumstance.
—*James A. Seddon to General Joseph E. Johnston, March 3, 1862*

With the closing of the Mississippi River to the Confederacy in July 1863, starving Rebel armies were forced to look to Florida for supplies of beef, corn, fish and pork. As Robert A. Taylor pointed out in *Rebel Storehouse: Florida in the Confederate Economy*, transporting quantities of pork and fish to armies hundreds of miles away took journeys of several weeks' duration. Salt was essential to preserving these foodstuffs as they moved northward and made their way to units in the field. The destruction of saltworks on the coasts of the Sunshine State and the loss of interior sources in Georgia and Tennessee to Union armies placed a severe strain on the ability of Confederates to preserve food supplies once they had been purchased or acquired.

As early as January 1863, General Robert E. Lee wrote to James A. Seddon, the Confederate secretary of war, about the plight of his Army of Northern Virginia when it came to provisions. "As far as I can learn, we have now about one week's supply, four days of fresh beef, and four days' salt meat, of the reduced rations. After that is exhausted, I know not whence further supplies can be drawn." Coming off an unsuccessful invasion of Maryland, but with an army that was still a potent offensive force, Lee's ability to maximize the effectiveness of his troops was hampered by the lack of a reliable source of rations for them. "The question of provisioning the army is becoming one of greater difficulty every day." He was opposed to the impressment of supplies because it would "produce aggravation and suffering among the people without much benefit to the army." Instead, Lee suggested that "if the citizens of the whole country were appealed to, they would be willing to restrict themselves and furnish what they have to the army." Although he was not concerned about the ability of the Army of Northern Virginia to fight and had no complaints about the supply of arms and munitions, Lee wrote Seddon that "I am more than usually anxious about the supplies of army, as it will be impossible to keep it together without food."

In 1863, Confederate armies were holding their own against superior Union armies, scoring several victories or draws on the battlefield. Union efforts to control the Mississippi River and split the Confederacy were in their early stages, and foodstuffs, principally cattle from Texas and the trans-Mississippi West, still flowed across the river into Rebel-held states. This would change with Grant's victory at Vicksburg on July 4, 1863. With the capture of that city, the river was closed to Confederate use, and cattle collected for shipment to Southern armies in the east languished on the western shore. Yankee gunboats made transporting beeves across the river in large numbers impossible.

Lee's request for additional provisions for his army was repeated by the commanders of other Confederate forces. Seddon and Confederate Commissary General Lucius Bellinger Northrop faced an impossible task in finding adequate sources of foodstuffs and ways to transport it to the armies. The lack of a viable transportation infrastructure in the Southern states that could supply large quantities of provisions to Rebel armies, plus the lack of sufficient warehouses for the supplies collected, created difficulties that were never overcome during the entire existence of the Confederacy. These difficulties were further exacerbated by the highly mobile campaigns fought by Southern armies as men and supplies were shifted to meet attacks by Union armies.

Even when adequate supplies were on hand, they frequently rotted before transportation could be found to ferry them to where they were needed. The failure of the central Confederate government to nationalize railroads or to standardize the gauge of railroad tracks imposed additional hardships. Railroad owners continued to operate their roads on a prewar model, often running two or more passenger trains for every train carrying freight because passengers paid in cash while fees for government shipments were paid haphazardly or not at all. On February 9, 1865, Lucius Northrop reported to John C. Breckinridge, who was now the Confederate secretary of war, that he had proposed to "stop all travel and private freight until our supplies were forwarded. This was promised by the Secretary [Seddon] in January, 1864, but not tried until March, when it was eminently successful." Enforcement of the policy was haphazard and never fully implemented. The failure of the central government to override private profit-making for the national good was a critical blow to gathering and forwarding requisitioned or purchased supplies for use by Confederate armies.

Lucius Bellinger Northrup, the Confederate commissary general, had the unenviable task of finding supplies for the armies of the Confederacy. He worked diligently, often to the accompanying abuse of his detractors, to get the job done. His persistence in procuring supplies from an economically prostrate Confederacy prolonged the war. *Original drawing by Jeanette Boughner. Courtesy of the Wynne Collection.*

As Federal armies moved into Southern states from the Mississippi River and southward from Kentucky, the Confederacy looked more and more to Florida to become the breadbasket of the South. By January 1863, Confederate military and civil authorities recognized that "Georgia and Florida are the only States east of the Mississippi with important supplies to spare," but unless the Confederate government undertook a program of railroad construction, available supplies would be lost because "planters are generally unable to carry their produce to the depots, and the railroads...are too deficient in rolling-stock to remove supplies as received."

There was no such thing as a standardized gauge for railroads—North and South—prior to the mid-1880s. Railroads varied from short-line tracks of a few miles' length to tracks that ran hundreds of miles. The gauge or width of the tracks was left up to the individual owners and could range from two feet in width for small, short lines to six feet wide for longer lines. What this meant for getting supplies from remote agricultural areas was that freight cars would sometimes have to be unloaded and loaded again several times before they reached their destination. Boxcars could not always be switched from one railroad to another. It was a problem that the Confederacy would never overcome.

Although Lee had opposed impressment as a way of finding supplies for the Southern armies, in March 1863, the informal impressment of food, fuel, slaves, animals and other commodities that were essential to the continued operations of military units began. On April 24, 1863, the Confederate Congress inaugurated a tax in kind, which required farmers to turn over 10 percent of all food and livestock produced and established a formal program of impressment. A complicated system of credits and payments for provisions was put in place, and a quartermaster was appointed to oversee collections in each congressional district in the Confederacy. The farmers and plantation owners in the South protested this tax as being onerous, burdensome and unfair. The payment schedule established by the central government did not take into consideration the rampant inflation that plagued the Confederate monetary system (in 1861, a Confederate dollar was valued at 90 percent of the United States dollar, but by 1863–64, the value had fallen to only seventeen cents when compared to the Union currency), nor did it consider the increased value of farm products and livestock due to the increasing scarcity of such items.

Confederate officials took note of the discord but, having no other recourse, continued with the impressment of supplies and the tax in kind. W.H. Johnston, the commissary general for Mississippi, noted in a communication on November 4, 1863, that "many hogs, it is thought, may be had from the counties bordering on the river, but Captain Chrisman is of the opinion that the prices authorized by the Government are so small that owners will not sell. Impressment must then be resorted to, and many of them will escape, as they will be driven off and hidden." Given the slowness of the Confederate Congress to appropriate funds for purchasing supplies, many procurement officials had to substitute promissory notes for cash, which many farmers refused to accept. As Confederate military fortunes waned in 1864 and 1865, the situation became desperate. On February 2, 1865, Major James

Fish, Corn and Citrus

Sloan, the chief commissary officer in North Carolina, reported to Northrop that "producers are refusing to sell, even at market prices, because they say the Government will not pay. Something should be done by the Treasury Department to meet the drafts which have been passed to their credit."

Seeking any reliable source of food for the armies of the Confederacy, Southern officials looked to the states of the lower South for fish in sufficient quantities to serve as a substitute for beef and pork. On January 24, 1864, Secretary Seddon approved a proposal by Lucius Northrop to reopen old fisheries closed by the naval blockade and to open new ones in the "rivers of Virginia and North Carolina, on the Gulf Coast, and at Mobile."

The best fishing grounds along the Florida coast were those along the banks and creeks of Apalachee Bay, St. Marks Bay and St. Andrews Bay, although waters near Tampa Bay proved to be productive as well. At Tampa, Captain James McKay, a prominent blockade runner and entrepreneur, established a large fishery to supply salted fish to the Confederacy. At St. Marks, slaves were used to work in the fisheries, and the same held true at fisheries on the Suwannee River, at St. Andrews and other fisheries along the Gulf shores. The presence of Union blockaders and the constant raids on saltworks after 1862 made life difficult for Florida fishermen, but by the end of 1864, 100,000 barrels of salted fish (or about twenty million pounds) made their way from the coast of Florida to the armies of the Confederacy. On August 12, 1864, Brigadier General John K. Jackson of the Military District of Florida confirmed this figure to the adjutant general and inspector general of the Confederate army, Samuel Cooper, and stated that it was likely that the production of fish in such quantities would continue annually if sufficient labor were "afforded" to the job. "The protection of these fisheries," he wrote, "devolves upon myself."

Although Confederates gained a significant victory over the Union army at Olustee on February 20, 1864, which blunted a Federal invasion from the east coast, David Levy Yulee wrote to his friend Jefferson Davis on July 31, 1864, about the necessity of stationing more Southern troops in the state to counteract the growing presence of Union forces on the west coast of Florida. Yulee, whose plantation was along the Crystal River, was clearly disturbed about the possibility that Union landing parties and army troops, along with deserters and Unionist bands, might destroy his property. He wrote:

> *The present invasion of Florida threatens, I think, the loss of the portion east of the Suwannee. It ought not to be lost if avoidable. Much force you cannot spare from the main points, but much force is not necessary. I think*

two good regiments, with the small force now here and the aid which a rally of our people can furnish, will answer. The effective force here is not now exceeding 800, I believe. The value of the peninsula is in the large supply of meats (beef and pork) which it supplies, and in its being the only region from which sugar and molasses are now furnished. Its extensive sea-coast of about 1,000 miles may become of great importance if the war is protracted in affording facilities for importations of necessary army supplies, and for its fisheries and salt.

The Confederate armies could not subsist on salted fish alone. Confederate subsistence agents scoured the countryside with a long list of supplies needed. At the top of their list was corn, which was needed to grind into meal for bread and for feed for the mules and horses the armies used. In the Sunshine State, thousands of acres of cotton and tobacco land were converted to growing corn as the price of this commodity, brought about by drought in other Southern states, rose from fifty cents a bushel to more than two dollars in 1861. Though Florida production of corn continued to rise during the next year, an inferior 1863 crop severely limited the amount available for home use and for export to the army and residents of other states. Only transfers of corn from government warehouses alleviated the need for subsistence. The failure of the 1863 corn crop was a harbinger of tougher times ahead.

Florida's contributions to easing the food shortages in the Confederate army, and the civilian population as well, were not limited to fish and corn. Scurvy was endemic in the Rebel army, and large shipments of oranges, lemons and limes were required to combat this disease caused by a vitamin C deficiency in the diets of soldiers. Floridians responded to the need for citrus by reactivating old abandoned groves and planting new ones. In addition, new stands of sugar cane were planted and harvested to produce syrup and sugar. Syrup was particularly desirable since Florida supply officers estimated that "100,000 gallons of sirup [*sic*]" had the nutritional value of four million pounds of bacon. General John K. Jackson noted that this amount of sugar and syrup "cannot, I believe, be supplied from any other portion of the country in our possession."

Although the Sunshine State produced great quantities of corn, fish, sugar, syrup and citrus, its hogs and cattle were the most highly valued of all its food supplies. The closure of the Mississippi River and the increasingly active Union army in Louisiana, Mississippi and Alabama prevented the shipping of hogs and cattle from these states to Confederate armies. Procurement officials looked to Florida to supply the needs of the nation.

Fish, Corn and Citrus

In reality, Florida produced little in the way of surplus hogs—indeed, barely enough to satisfy the demands for this staple of the Southern diet by the white and slave residents of the state. Pork was so scarce in the state in 1861 that, according to historian Robert A. Taylor, "the state government had to seek outside Florida for pork products to feed the regiments then being raised...[and] troops on the peninsula subsisted on hams imported from as far away as Charleston and Wilmington, North Carolina." Despite efforts to boost pork production in the Sunshine State, the failure of corn crops meant that there was little in the way of feed for hogs. Nevertheless, Confederate officials and civilians from other states persisted in visiting Florida in search of pork.

Although the overall production of pork declined in Florida, commissary agents remained convinced that pork was plentiful in the state. Brigadier General John K. Jackson reported to General Samuel Cooper as late as August 1864 that the counties in the central portion of the state could produce "10,000 head of hogs, equal to 1,000,000 pounds of bacon," annually.

As the landmass of the Confederate states shrank and the Union blockade was strengthened, securing enough provisions to feed its armies and civilian populations proved to be increasingly difficult. Although General Jackson proudly proclaimed in 1864, "The peninsula of Florida, presenting as it does quite one-half of the coast of the Confederate States, affords great opportunities for evading the enemy's blockaders, and bringing in supplies for the Government," the reality was that the scale of Rebel needs was so great and the number of successful runs through the blockade was so small that this was unrealistic. Even if the number of successful runs had doubled or even tripled, it is highly unlikely that whatever supplies brought in would have made it out of the Sunshine State to places north.

Chapter 12

Cattle, Contrabands and Conflict

I propose to establish a small post on Charlotte Harbor to enlist the men above referred to, as many as possible, to break up or check the cattle-driving business in that part of the State, and to extend operations according to circumstances. Nineteen men, refugees from the State of Florida, now residing at this place, have recently enlisted in the service of the United States, and as many more will probably enlist unconditionally, but with the understanding that their first service shall be in the State of Florida.

As we have but one regiment of troops in this district, the Forty-seventh Pennsylvania, divided between Key West and Tortugas, it will, of course, be impossible to detach any considerable force. I propose to detach one company only of the Forty-seventh Pennsylvania to act in conjunction with the native troops. The native troops propose to take the name of the Florida Rangers.

—Brigadier Daniel P. Woodbury, Key West, Florida, December 23, 1863

By late 1863, the Union blockading squadron along Florida's coasts was firmly in place, and commanders slowly began to expand the mission of the fleet. As George E. Buker points out in *Blockaders, Refugees & Contrabands: Civil War on Florida's Gulf Coast, 1861–1865*, naval officers had early on adopted a policy of establishing friendly contact with Unionists and contrabands on the mainland, and this policy would pay dividends as the Federal army finally decided to move into the Sunshine State. Although Union army troops had occupied Fernandina, St. Augustine and, on several occasions, Jacksonville on the Atlantic Coast since 1861, they had made no significant advances into the interior of the state. Baldwin, the railroad hub west of Jacksonville, was the limit of their activities, although periodic incursions into the St. Johns River by Union forces met stiff resistance from Confederate forces commanded by Captain J.J. Dickison.

In December 1863, General Daniel P. Woodbury, the commander of Union army forces in Key West, decided to undertake the organization of Florida Unionists, contrabands and Confederate deserters into a force he could use to bring the Gulf Coast entirely under Federal control. The Union navy had given protection to contrabands and Unionists and had created several camps to house them. These camps were a source of men for Woodbury's proposed new force, and he was also optimistic that he could readily field new army units from the "deserters from the rebel army and men hiding to avoid conscription...lurking in the woods between Charlotte Harbor and Lake Okeechobee, in numbers variously estimated from 200 or 300 to 700 or 800, and that many of these men would join the forces of the United States should a military post be established in their neighborhood." With the support of Admiral Theodorus Bailey, commander of the East Gulf Blockading Squadron who promised to use his ships to provide protection for the fort, and the approval of Major General Nathaniel P. Banks, commander of the Union Army of the Gulf, Woodbury began to carry out his plan.

Woodbury's initial objective was to disrupt the flow of the "two thousand head of cattle [that] are reported to be driven out of Florida every week for the use of the rebel armies." In approving the plan, General Banks cautioned against "any surprise by the enemy" and ordered that any "movement should be of a temporary character." Banks further admonished him that "if the supply of beef be of importance to our army, a force should be sent there sufficiently large to scour the country." He agreed that Woodbury could "pursue any operations that he may consider safe, but under no circumstances should he place his command where it can be surprised or overpowered."

Fort Myers, a Seminole Indian War fort opposite Punta Rassa on the Caloosahatchee River, was occupied by a detachment of the Forty-seventh Pennsylvania Cavalry, and Enoch Daniels, a refugee from the navy camp on Useppa Island, accompanied them. Daniels was allowed to "communicate freely with people living on the mainland" to recruit Unionists for service in the Florida Refugee Rangers, an irregular volunteer force that would carry out raids in the interior. Once Daniels had enlisted eighty men, he would be appointed as a captain or first lieutenant to command these irregulars.

On December 17, 1864, Daniels was ordered to take a small armed detachment to begin his recruitment drive. Woodbury established four goals for the operation. First, Daniels would "afford Union men in the State of

With the surrender of Vicksburg on July 4, 1863, the Mississippi River was closed to Confederate commerce. The vast cattle herds of Texas could no longer be shuttled across the river to waiting Confederate armies. The small, scrawny cattle of the Florida prairies became the primary source of fresh beef for Rebel soldiers. *Courtesy of the Wynne Collection.*

Florida an opportunity to enlist in the service of the United States." Second, he and his men would "break up or check the cattle-driving business in the neighborhood of Charlotte Harbor and as far north as practicable." Third, he would "procure able-bodied negroes [*sic*] for the service of the United States." Last, the Rangers would "obtain cattle for the use of the United States." The Rangers, Woodbury ordered, would "be governed by the laws of war and by the regulations of the War Department," which included the confiscation of the property of men "in arms against the United States." Under no circumstances would the person or property of peaceable citizens be injured, nor would women and children be disturbed.

On December 23, 1863, just a week after he requested a commission for Daniels, Woodbury filed another request to Banks's headquarters asking that Daniels's appointment to command the Rangers be suspended and that Acting Master's Mate Henry A. Crane, who had demonstrated his leadership skills in naval operations in the Indian River, be transferred from the blockading squadron and commissioned as a captain to command the Rangers. Woodbury's decision to replace Daniels as the captain of the

Rangers was made even before Daniels led an ill-fated raid up the Myakka River on Christmas Day. Crane received a provisional appointment to captain of the Rangers.

Crane, who had previous army experience as a colonel in the Florida militia and had refused a commission as lieutenant colonel in the Confederate army, was recommended by Admiral Bailey. According to Woodbury, Crane enjoyed "the full confidence of Admiral Bailey and of all the naval officers who have had occasion to notice him during the past year." In February 1864, Crane's appointment as captain of the Rangers was returned to General Banks, and he was commissioned as a captain in the newly formed Second Florida Cavalry, a regular army unit. The Second Florida, made up of white Unionists and Confederate deserter recruits, would serve until the end of the war.

Florida cattle were essential to the continued survival of Confederate armies in the field—so essential that a special Confederate cavalry unit, the First Battalion Florida Special Cavalry, was organized in late 1863 under the command of Major (later Colonel) Charles J. Munnerlyn. This unit would collect cattle for the commissary department, herd them to railheads in south Georgia and protect them against raids by Rangers and Union troops operating out of Fort Myers and the predatory bands of deserters and outlaws that lurked in the swamps and forests along the way north.

How many cattle the Confederacy could possibly gain from Florida was an open question. By the beginning of 1864, all available beeves from north Florida, including many milk cows, had been collected and sent north. The state comptroller of Florida reported in 1862 that the Sunshine State was home to 658,609 cattle, up from the 1860 census estimate of 388,060. South Florida was reported to have enough beeves to supply all the Confederate armies. When he took up his position as chief commissary agent for Florida, Major Pleasant W. White indicated that his bureau would be able to supply 4,000 head per month. White's estimate was grossly inflated, and Florida was never able to supply this number of cattle because of a lack of transportation and because of Yankee raids.

Florida cattle were generally classified as "scrub" cattle, descended from the small, rangy, lean cattle of the Spanish and allowed to feed only on the grasses of the Florida prairies. Though the cattle were adapted to this kind of environment, they had very little fat on their bones and produced little in the way of desirable meat. Yet they were the sole source of beef in the Confederacy and could supply meat—even if it was tough and tasteless—to troops that had no meat rations at all. Fattening Florida cattle would involve feeding them on nutrient-rich grass in northern pastures for an extended period of time—time the Confederacy did not have. Long cattle drives further reduced the nutritional value of such cattle. Attempts to slaughter them before they left Florida and pack them in salt for shipment to Southern armies met with little success. When Major White tried to do this in Jackson County, he discovered that there were not enough barrels to pack the salted beef in, nor were there materials or coopers available to make them. White's efforts produced fewer results than he had promised.

Along the trail drive, representatives of private businesses, agents of other government agencies, purchasing agents for states and cities and private consumers sought to purchase cattle, alive or pickled, at higher prices than the central government would pay. The end result of this competition was that the number of Florida cattle or barrels of salted beef that actually reached soldiers in the field was very small. On August 12, 1864, Brigadier General John K. Jackson, the subsistence officer for the Military District of Florida, promised to deliver twenty-five thousand head of cattle—"equal to 10,000,000 pounds"—to the army if the Confederate government would supply five thousand troops to guard the state's railroads and to lay additional tracks to connect with Georgia railroads. Like Major White, Jackson's promises proved illusory.

The raids on cattle herds made by the Union troops stationed at Fort Myers made collecting and protecting herds of cattle by Confederate drivers and troops difficult. The Second Florida Cavalry, led by Captain Henry Crane, would soon have a total of more than 750 men. It was bolstered by the Second Infantry Regiment of United States Colored Troops, which had been assigned to Fort Myers. These troops carried out a number of raids on the cattle-rich areas around Fort Meade, and this action disrupted the efforts of the Confederate cow cavalry to round up and push beeves north.

The mission of the Union blockading ships changed as the Federal army expanded its operations. No longer concerned only with stopping blockade runners, the fleet now undertook combined operations with the army, transporting men and animals to points along the Gulf for operations in the interior. Sailors were given additional responsibilities—much like those of marines—of establishing temporary land bases and acting as guards to protect the rear of invading army units. On July 25, 1864, Acting Master James J. Russell of the USS *Ariel* reported a typical combined army-navy expedition to raid Brooksville and Bayport in Hernando County that began on July 7. With 250 soldiers under the command of Captain J.W. Childs, the *Ariel*, along with the schooners *Stonewall*, *Rosalie* and *Sea Bird*, proceeded to the north side of the Anclote River and disembarked the soldiers. The *Ariel* and the *Sea Bird* then proceeded to Bayport, which they found to be deserted. After the raid on Brooksville, the Union troops met the ships at Bayport, and on July 13, all the soldiers, plus two Confederate deserters, were aboard the ships and bound for Tampa Bay.

The Brooksville expedition was not the only joint operation undertaken by the Union navy and units of the army. The previous May, the navy bark *James L. Davis* and the gunboat *Honduras* had provided transportation for units of the Second Florida Cavalry and the Second Infantry Regiment to attack Tampa. In addition, thirty men from the *Davis* were part of the Federal attacking force that successfully invaded the town and destroyed Fort Brooke and the cannons in place there. Similar cooperative raids were conducted at Cedar Key and St. Marks in 1864 and 1865.

Perhaps the best known of the army-navy combined operations in Florida came on March 4, 1865. Brigadier General John Newton, who had replaced Woodbury in command of the Union army in south Florida (Woodbury died of yellow fever in August 1864), launched an attack from St. Marks and set out to follow the St. Marks River to Tallahassee. With the assistance of Admiral C.K. Stribling, who was the new commander of the East Gulf Blockading Squadron and made a number of his ships available for transport and protection, Newton's force included men from the Second Infantry Regiment and the Ninety-ninth Infantry Regiment, both units of the United States Colored Troops. The Second Florida Cavalry and a battery of two howitzers manned by Union sailors completed his force. He met Confederate resistance first near the St. Marks Lighthouse, where a small force under the command of Governor John Milton's son, Major William H. Milton, delayed the Union landing. News of the invasion force was hurriedly sent to Tallahassee, where Generals Samuel Jones and William Miller assembled a force of Confederate regulars, men home on leave or in transit to their regular units, local militia and even cadets from a nearby military school to meet the Yankees.

On March 5, Newton encountered the makeshift Confederate force at the East River Bridge and drove them back to the Newport Bridge, where a smaller Confederate force was entrenched. Unable to dislodge this group, he looked for another route of attack. His scouts reported that he could cross the river at Natural Bridge a few miles up the river. Abandoning his attack at Newport Bridge, Newton ordered his troops to march rapidly to this crossing. Generals Jones and Miller realized his intention and sent their forces racing to defend Natural Bridge. The Confederates won the foot race, and when Newton's troops arrived, they found the Rebel forces in place and waiting.

Throughout the morning of March 6, the Union troops launched attack after attack. Although the fighting was intense and involved heavy exchanges of small arms and artillery fire, the Union efforts were defeated. Despite taking some losses, Confederate forces grew stronger and stronger during the day as reinforcements poured in from surrounding areas. At the end of the day, Newton realized he had lost and ordered a full retreat back to St. Marks and the safety of the batteries of the Union fleet. Tallahassee was saved and so, too, was the possible invasion of southwestern Georgia.

Newton's defeat followed closely on the heels of a thrust at Tallahassee made by Brigadier General Alexander Asboth the previous September, when he had led a force of seven hundred Union cavalry and infantry troops from Pensacola into the Panhandle. Asboth's force managed to get as far as Marianna before being forced to turn back by Confederate forces. Asboth was wounded in the attack but deemed it a success since his units had defeated a Rebel cavalry force under the command of Colonel Montgomery. Asboth reported to General Banks that his troops had captured Montgomery and "80 of his men, 200 horses and mules, 100 stand[s] of arms, several wagons, 400 cattle, and 600 contrabands, all of which were brought safely within our lines." Union losses were thirty-nine soldiers killed, wounded and missing.

The loss of slaves, either through capture or by defection to Union forces, had a serious impact on the Florida economy. Reports filed by ships' captains as they raided coastal installations in Florida seldom fail to mention contrabands being taken on board. Official navy policy was to encourage contrabands to flee areas of the South, and early in the war, Union secretary of the navy Gideon Welles allowed them to be recruited into naval service. Contrabands taken in Florida were used in a variety of tasks, including performing manual labor at naval installations. Those who did not join the navy were housed in refugee camps and provided food, clothing and shelter by the navy. This policy of generous treatment paid enormous intelligence dividends for the navy. The loss of slaves, many of whom were experienced fishermen or salt workers, further reduced the ability of Floridians to contribute supplies to Confederate forces.

Once the Union army arrived in force in the Sunshine State, it, too, followed the same basic policy, and the use of African American troops by the army encouraged slaves to flee in greater numbers. By war's end, some 1,044 Florida contrabands had joined Union regiments.

Chapter 13

The Final Year

1865

SIR: On the evening of the 1ˢᵗ instant an aid of General Sherman arrived here with information that Jefferson Davis and Cabinet, with considerable treasure, passed Charlotte, N.C., on the 23d ultimo, escorted by a large cavalry force, and that it was supposed they would attempt to make their escape from the coast of east or west Florida. To-day I received a dispatch from Admiral Dahlgren giving me the same information. I dispatched a vessel to the west coast yesterday morning to give the information and ordered all fishing and other boats from this place to return immediately to Key West. The vessels at the blockaded ports will remain at their stations and all cruising vessels have been ordered to guard with vigilance the coast, and, if possible, prevent the escape of the rebels. I also sent off yesterday two boat expeditions to cruise inside the reef and amongst the keys to Cape Florida.

I have to-day ordered an expedition under Commander Cooper to take possession of Key Biscayne and to guard the passage to the Gulf from it and Bear's Cut to the eastward of the key. It is not improbable the rebels may attempt to leave the United States by one of these inlets, as there is a land route to Fort Dallas, at the mouth of the Miami River. All that region of Florida is well known by Mr. Mallory. I think we shall be able to prevent their escape from any place they can reach in this vicinity. The west coast will be more difficult to guard, from its great extent. Admiral Dahlgren has sent a number of vessels along the east coast, and I have requested him (he offered to do so) to guard the coast from Key Biscayne, as we had not vessels enough to do it and guard other parts of the coast.

I have the honor to be, very respectfully, your obedient servant,
Admiral C. K. Stribling to Secretary of the Navy Gideon Welles
HDQRS. EAST GULF BLOCKADING SQUADRON,
Key West, Fla., May 3, 1865

C onfederate hopes for defeating the Union were gone by the beginning of 1865, but a slim hope remained that it might be possible to reach a negotiated settlement that would allow the Southern nation to continue to exist. General Robert E. Lee and the Army of Northern Virginia, now barely thirty-five thousand strong and suffering from a lack of supplies, manned a line from Richmond to St. Petersburg, holding the large Federal army of General Ulysses S. Grant at bay. Too weak to launch offensive operations, Lee waited for the inevitable onslaught that would spell the end of the Confederacy's capital. In Tennessee, General John Bell Hood, having lost Atlanta to Sherman the year before, seemed intent on destroying his Army of Tennessee in futile confrontations with Union armies. General Joseph E. Johnston was brought out of exile in February 1865 and replaced Hood. His command, which numbered about thirty thousand troops, had the onerous task of opposing Union general William Tecumseh Sherman, who took Savannah in December 1864 and moved into South Carolina in early 1865. Union attacks in other sections of the Confederacy tied down the small formations of state troops that might have been used to bolster the two major Confederate armies.

With the borders of the Confederacy shrinking every day, there were still those who thought the Southern nation could be salvaged—perhaps through negotiations, such as the Hampton Roads Peace Conference in February 1865, or through the intervention of France and Prussia with fresh troops. A few diehards argued that fighting a guerrilla war in the mountainous states of the Confederacy might continue the struggle for years, but this was not acceptable to the officers of the army. Following the collapse of Confederate defenses at Petersburg and Richmond, Jefferson Davis and some of his cabinet made their

With the collapse of Petersburg and Richmond, Confederate president Jefferson Davis made his way south, along with several members of his cabinet, to find a way to join General Edmund Kirby-Smith in the Confederate Trans-Mississippi West and continue the war. *Courtesy of the Library of Congress.*

way south, first to Danville, Virginia, and then to Washington, Georgia. At a final council of war Davis held with the remaining members of his government who were present in Georgia, he indicated his intention of escaping to the Department of the Trans-Mississippi West, where the army of General Edmund Kirby-Smith still controlled vast areas of territory. Using this as a new base of operations, Davis felt certain he could reach a negotiated settlement with the United States that would allow the preservation of the Confederacy.

Davis, who was aware that he was being pursued by Union troops, set off on his journey south as soon as the war council was over. With his aide-de-camp, his wife and John H. Reagan, who had been appointed Confederate secretary of the treasury on April 27, he made his way toward the Florida coast, where he hoped to find passage aboard a blockade runner that would take him to Texas.

General Edmund Kirby-Smith, a Florida native, commanded the Department of the Trans-Mississippi West, where the Confederacy's largest army was still a viable fighting force. With the capture of Davis, Kirby-Smith surrendered on May 26, 1865. *Courtesy of the Florida Photographic Archives.*

Other members of his cabinet—Stephen R. Mallory and John C. Breckinridge—left the Davis party and set out on their own. Mallory, who submitted his formal resignation before departing, made his way to La Grange, Georgia, where he joined his wife and children. Breckinridge, who had been a vice president of the United States, a Confederate general and the last Confederate secretary of war and who feared possible Federal prosecution for treason if captured, decided to work his way down the eastern coast of Florida in the hopes of reaching safety in Cuba.

Judah P. Benjamin, who was the last Confederate secretary of state, left the Davis party before it reached Washington, Georgia, and also made plans to flee the American continent. Traveling alone under an assumed name, he made his way through Georgia to Ocala, Florida, where he stayed with a relative for a few days before moving farther south to the Gamble mansion in

Left: John C. Breckinridge was an antebellum Union army officer and politician. He served one term as vice president of the United States. When war came in 1861, he cast his lot with the Confederacy. After active service in several theaters, he became the last Rebel secretary of war in early 1865. *Courtesy of the Library of Congress.*

Below: Gamble Mansion, near Ellington, Florida, was one of Judah P. Benjamin's resting places as he made his way down the coast of Florida. The mansion, built by Major Robert Gamble, still stands and is operated as a state park. *Courtesy of the Florida Photographic Archives.*

Ellington. From there, he was able to secure passage to Bimini on a small boat, thence to Nassau and on to Great Britain. Benjamin, a former U.S. senator from Louisiana, was suspected by Union officials as being the mastermind behind the shooting of Abraham Lincoln on April 14, a suspicion that he felt he could never successfully refute in a Yankee court.

The next day, April 28, General Joseph E. Johnston surrendered his Army of Tennessee to General William T. Sherman at Bennett Place, North Carolina. Union pleasure at the surrender of Generals Lee and Johnston was dampened by grief at the shooting of Abraham Lincoln by actor John Wilkes Booth. Booth was pursued and killed by Union troops on April 26. The assassination of Lincoln was roundly condemned by Generals Lee and Johnston, and many Southerners who might have been disposed to continue their struggle against the United States decried this "unmanly act" and accepted defeat. Southern prisoners of war, still held in camps in the North, were worried that the Union soldiers would exact revenge against them. Hiram Smith Williams, who had been captured at the Battle of Bentonville a few days before Johnston's surrender and was sent to the Point Lookout, Maryland prison, noted in his diary on April 16, "3,000 men to be drawn for and shot in this prison as retaliation."

Messages were dispatched from Union generals Grant and Sherman to all Union commands alerting them to Davis's flight. On April 26, Grant sent a telegram to Union secretary of war Edwin M. Stanton with the news that "Jeff Davis, with his Cabinet, passed into South Carolina, with the intention, no doubt, of getting out of the country, either via Cuba or across the Mississippi. Sherman sent this information via Wilmington, yesterday to Admiral Dahlgren and General [Quincy Adams] Gillmore for them to be on the watch. I think it would be advisable to give the same information to the naval commanders on the Mississippi River and all post commanders."

Along the Mississippi River, Federal gunboats cruised the shores, confiscating all boats that could be used to cross the river and watching the banks for any signs of the fleeing Confederate president. Union cavalry units roamed the countryside searching for any sign of Davis and his party. Speculation about where he was headed was rampant, and there was a great deal of concern that the Confederate ram *Stonewall* had been ordered to break the blockade and pick up the Davis party at some point along the Florida coast. On April 28, Gideon Welles alerted Admiral C.K. Stribling, the commander of the East Gulf Blockading Squadron:

> *Information has been received from the U.S. consul at Teneriffe* [sic] *to the effect that the rebel ram* Stonewall *left that place, where she obtained*

a supply of coal, April 1 at 6 p.m. and steamed away rapidly to the south. Her destination is believed to be some point on our coast, and every precaution should be taken by you to guard against surprise and to prevent her inflicting serious injury should she make her appearance anywhere within the limits of your command, and the best means in your power used to capture or destroy her.

Admiral Samuel Phillips Lee, who commanded the Mississippi River Squadron, ordered his flotilla into action. On April 28, he reported to Gideon Welles that "the chief of Major-General [John] Pope's staff has gone up Red River in a gunboat furnished by me, to propose to General Kirby Smith, by General Pope's order, the terms of surrender allowed by General Grant to General Lee. Should this offer be accepted, the rebellion is at an end, even if Jeff. Davis succeeds in reaching the Trans-Mississippi Department."

On May 3, 1865, Admiral Stribling notified Welles that a member of General Sherman's staff had arrived in Key West on May 1 with news that Davis and his cabinet were on their way south and "that it was supposed they would attempt to make their escape from the coast of east or west Florida." To prevent that, he reported, he had "ordered all fishing and other boats from this place to return immediately to Key West. The vessels at the blockaded ports will remain at their stations and all cruising vessels have been ordered to guard with vigilance the coast, and, if possible, prevent the escape of the rebels. I also sent off yesterday two boat expeditions to cruise inside the reef and amongst the keys to Cape Florida." In addition, he "ordered an expedition under Commander Cooper to take possession of Key Biscayne and to guard the passage to the Gulf from it and Bear's Cut to the eastward of the key. It is not improbable the rebels may attempt to leave the United States by one of these inlets, as there is a land route to Fort Dallas, at the mouth of the Miami River." Finally, he reported that Admiral John A.B. Dahlgren, the commander of the South Atlantic Blockading Squadron, had dispatched ships to help seal off the eastern coast of the Sunshine State.

For more than two weeks, Union forces searched for Jefferson Davis. As Federal cavalry units scoured the country from the Carolinas to Mississippi looking for any signs of him, Union naval vessels stepped up their patrols along the coasts of the former Confederacy and the rivers of the region. Citizens of the United States and the Confederacy waited anxiously for news about the Confederate president.

Finally, the news came that troops of Major General James Harrison Wilson's Michigan cavalry had surprised the Davis party on May 10 at

Irwinville, Georgia, and taken them as prisoners. On May 16, General George H. Thomas notified Admiral Lee:

General Wilson has reported to me officially that Jeff. Davis and family; Reagan, Postmaster-General, C.S., and Colonel Harrison, private secretary; Colonel Johnston, aid-de-camp; and others of Davis's personal staff were captured at Irwinville, Ga., on the morning of the 10th at daylight. Clement C. Clay delivered himself to Wilson on the 12th at Macon, and A.H. Stephens was arrested by General Upton on the 11th at Augusta. Governor Brown, of Georgia, was also arrested by Wilson on the 4th instant. So it seems the Southern Confederacy and Georgia are done for.

On May 27, Welles received word that "on the morning of the 21st of May, Acting Rear-Admiral Stribling received official dispatches announcing the surrender of the rebel pirate ram *Stonewall* to the Spanish authorities in Havana." The last major threat to Union vessels of the blockade had been removed. News of the *Stonewall's* surrender was quickly followed by the news that

Brigadier General James Harrison Wilson and his Michigan cavalry captured Jefferson Davis at the small Georgia town of Irwinville on May 10, 1865. Wilson was immediately promoted to major general. *Courtesy of the Library of Congress.*

General [John] *Newton, commanding the army forces at Key West, received information that his pickets at Cape Sable, had captured a boat containing 7 white persons and 1 colored, all armed, and to appearance, persons of importance. They had embarked at Crystal River, pulling and sailing along the coast of Florida during the night, and secreting themselves during the day. Their object was to get to Havana. They gave their names as follows: Frank C. Anderson, Frederick Moh[l]e, Richard S. McCullock, Thomas A. Harris, Julius C. Pratt, Isaac A. Homer, Henry W. McCormick. Not having been received at Key West, it is not known who they are. Their conduct looks suspicious and leads to the supposition that they were men of importance in the so-called Confederacy, and that many of the names given are fictitious. It is thought Breckinridge and Mallory, are among them.*

The *New York Times* published an extended report on May 28, 1865, which added to the speculation. Although the men "all acknowledge to have recently been in Richmond," the *Times* could not add any more information. The speculation that John C. Breckinridge and Stephen R. Mallory were part of the group was erroneous, however. Mallory had already been captured at La Grange, while Breckinridge was successfully making his way to Cuba along the east coast.

John C. Breckinridge, who had served as secretary of state for the Confederate States of America government, was fleeing across the South with a handful of men. When Breckinridge reached Florida in June, he was aided by Captain J.J. Dickison, who had commanded the Second Florida Cavalry and had been known as "Florida's Gray Ghost," an allusion to his ability to strike and then vanish.

Dickison helped Breckinridge and his party move through Florida, south along the St. Johns River and then overland to the Indian River south of Titusville. From there, the Southern leader and his men rowed down the long lagoon, avoiding Union naval patrols afloat and cavalry on the shore. They rowed past a Union camp at the Indian River Inlet (north of the present-day Fort Pierce Inlet) during one dark night and hauled their longboat across the southern part of Jupiter Island into the Atlantic Ocean on June 4, 1865. A few miles to the south, the fleeing Confederates managed to capture a schooner and sail to exile in Cuba, then to South America and England.

General Edmund Kirby-Smith surrendered the last remaining Confederate army and the Trans-Mississippi West to Union authorities on May 26. He then fled to Mexico. The war was over.

J.J. Dickison, Florida's famed "Swamp Fox," commanded Confederate troops along the St. Johns River. After the war, Dickison wrote the volume of history on the operation of Confederate troops in Florida and served as the commander of the state's Confederate Veterans organization. *Courtesy of the Florida Photographic Archives.*

The East Coast Blockading Squadron continued its patrols along Florida's coasts for a few more days. On May 31, however, Admiral Stribling received orders to "reduce the East Gulf Squadron to the following number of *vessels* with all possible dispatch, viz: Four tugboats, ten other *steamers*. You can have in addition such store vessels as may be required in connection with this force." Similar orders were sent to the other squadrons. The Union, which had expended millions of dollars in building and buying ships to enforce the blockade, was now in a hurry to downsize as quickly as possible. No longer at war, the Navy Department also embarked on a campaign to reduce expenses, and Stribling, who was instructed to send the bulk of his fleet to Boston and Philadelphia, was ordered to "economize in the use of coal and give directions to all vessels to keep steam down, except in an emergency, of which the senior officer shall judge, under the directions of the commander of the squadron."

A fitting epitaph for what had become the greatest navy in the world.

Chapter 14

The End

U.S.S. HIBISCUS
Cedar Keys, April 16, 1865

SIR: I have the honor to report the capture of the rebel sloop boat Florida, *with 5 persons on board and a cargo of cotton, also the rebel sloop boat* Annie, *with 2 persons on board and a quantity of loose cotton. These captures were made on the morning of the 11ᵗʰ of April, off Crystal River, by the U.S. schooner* Sea Bird, *tender to this vessel, Acting Master E.L. Robbins in command. Both vessels, in my opinion, being unfit to send to Key West, I have taken everything of value on board this vessel and destroyed the vessels and will send their cargoes and the prisoners to Key West by first opportunity. Enclosed please find list of the names of all the persons attached to this vessel at the time of the capture.*

Very respectfully, your obedient servant,
WM. L. MARTINE
Acting Volunteer Lieutenant, Commanding

Historians are split in their opinions of the overall impact of the Union blockade on the failure of the Confederate States to win the Civil War. Some argue that the loss of some 1,500 blockade runners to blockading squadrons prevented equipping the Rebel army with enough arms, munitions and other military paraphernalia to offset the material advantages the Union army possessed because of the industrial supremacy of the United States. Although such shortages did exist occasionally, reports from Confederate commanders in the field downplay scarcities of equipment and point to shortages of food, clothing and shoes. Although blockade runners brought in vast quantities of these items, the real problem faced by the Confederacy was the lack of manufacturing concerns to produce them within the borders of the Southern nation. To some extent, the South overcame these obstacles, although food, clothing and shoes remained in short supply.

The blockade was instrumental in preventing the Confederate states from exporting enough cotton and other agricultural products to wield a great deal of influence in European markets. The central government of the Confederacy thought that an embargo on the export of cotton and tobacco would be enough to force other nations to grant recognition to the infant nation. The embargo on Southern cotton, however, produced two detrimental effects on the Confederacy. First, manufacturing nations quickly found alternative sources—India, Egypt and North Africa—of the staple, and the much-hoped-for shortages did not occur. By the time the South resumed exporting cotton, adequate supplies for European mills had arrived, and the projected shortages did not happen.

The early reliance by the Confederacy on "King Cotton" diplomacy also had a second undesired result. One historian has estimated that the blockade and the self-imposed embargo reduced the revenue available to the South by some $700 million. The most significant result of this lost revenue was the inability of Confederate purchase agents in Europe to buy enough first-class naval vessels to lift the blockade. Given the poor quality of the ships that enforced the blockade, even a few well-armed vessels could have made a difference. As it was, the warships brought into Confederate service operated on the periphery of the war, acting as commerce raiders but never seriously threatening the Union blockading squadrons. Perhaps a few well-planned and executed raids on Northern ports would have been enough—particularly when combined with the successes of Rebel armies during 1861 and 1862—to force the Union to seek a negotiated peace.

The imposition of the blockade and the failure of the Confederacy to seriously challenge it also hampered the ability of the South to expand the reach of its armies through water-borne assaults. The Union, on the other hand, made good use of its blockading ships and riverine fleet to carry out the Anaconda Plan to isolate the South. Along the Mississippi River network, Union gunboats not only shelled Confederate installations but also protected other vessels carrying troops to attack Rebel fortifications or to launch new attacks. The failure of the Confederacy to do this curtailed the mobility of Confederate armies.

Psychologically, the blockade paid tremendous dividends in breaking Confederate morale. Although much of the cargo carried in the holds of blockade runners was made up of luxury items that only the rich could afford, all Southerners suffered the loss of simple household items that had traditionally been imported from Northern states or from Europe. Needles, pins, thimbles, medicines and hundreds of other items simply disappeared from the marketplace or were so costly that the average person could not afford them.

Floridians had to cope with other problems created by the blockade. The aggressive approach of blockading ships in attacking saltworks and fisheries while on blockade duty not only prevented goods from flowing in and out of the peninsula but also destroyed valuable sources of food and salt. Thus, the losses of Floridians were compounded. The constant flow of contrabands to blockading ships and, after 1863, to Union army units had an impact on the productivity of Florida farms and plantations. With the closing of the Mississippi River in the summer of 1863 and the unreliable imports of blockade runners, Confederate authorities looked to Florida for foodstuffs to supply the Rebel armies, factory labor forces and cities of the northern Confederacy. Impressment agents, commissary officers and speculators scoured the Florida countryside, taking or buying every available food they could find. Common people faced starvation, which dampened their enthusiasm for the Confederacy. Countless letters to men serving in the Rebel armies attest to the impoverished lives of women and children on the homefront.

As conditions worsened, Floridians faced additional dangers from Unionists, emboldened by the constant presence of blockading ships on the coasts, who joined with Confederate deserters and runaway slaves to raid isolated homesteads and villages. The narrow peninsula also meant that the heartland of Florida was vulnerable to incursions by the combined Union naval and army forces. Although Floridians managed to blunt the larger invasions from Pensacola, Jacksonville and along the coast, the reality was that the Union forces used in these campaigns were small in number. The threat of something more was always present.

Was the blockade of Florida successful? Yes and no. It wasn't particularly efficient in stopping the hundreds of small blockade runners that moved in and out of the estuaries and rivers along Florida's coasts, but it did prevent large shipments of cotton and agricultural products from leaving the Sunshine State. Its greatest success, however, was the tremendous pressure—economic and psychological—it placed on the population of the state. Living with the constant threat of "what might happen" paid dividends for the Union war effort.

By 1865, war weariness and years of deprivation had exacted a heavy toll. Although Floridians of later generations would take great pride in the fact that Florida's capital was never conquered and that the Sunshine State did not surrender until May 10, 1865, the simple fact was that Confederate Florida was an exhausted house of cards, waiting for a single push to collapse.

Additional Reading

The physical limitations imposed by the publisher (forty thousand words) makes an in-depth examination of some aspects of this topic impossible, but exploring the question of the Union blockade of the Confederate coast and of Florida in particular leads to a number of previously published works by a number of historians. Researchers have a broad base of solid scholarship to draw on to flesh out their knowledge of this topic. Many of these works are somewhat dated, but the overall level of investigation is excellent. Periodically, historians need to reexamine important questions and bring them once again to new audiences. We hope we have done that in this volume.

To fully understand the ramifications of the blockade on the Sunshine State, the first book that should be consulted is George E. Buker's *Blockaders, Refugees and Contrabands: Civil War on Florida's Gulf Coast, 1861–1865* (University of Alabama Press, 1993). Buker has provided an excellent look at how the Union took advantage of the splits in the state's society to mobilize small forces of white Unionists, deserters and contrabands to disrupt wartime activities and to undertake incursions into the center of the Florida peninsula. Buker's book is the mandatory first step for any researcher interested in the topic.

Robert A. Taylor's *Rebel Storehouse: Florida in the Confederate Economy* (University of Alabama Press, 1995) takes a hard look at how Florida was perceived as the Confederacy's breadbasket after the loss of Vicksburg in mid-1863. His thorough use of the papers of Florida's commissary general, Major Pleasant W. White, his reliance on extant newspaper sources, his use of personal diaries and his adroit use of the *Official Records* make *Rebel Storehouse* a Florida classic.

For an easy-to-read overall view of the Sunshine State and its role in this great American conflict, consult Lewis N. Wynne and Robert A. Taylor's *Florida in the Civil War* (Arcadia Publishing, 2001).

David G. Surdam authored *Northern Naval Superiority and the Economics of the American Civil War* (University of South Carolina, 2001), which presents an economic analysis of the impact of blockade and points out what might have happened if the Confederacy had dedicated more resources to lifting the blockade. Stephen R. Wise's *Lifeline of the Confederacy: Blockade Running During the Civil War* (University of South Carolina Press, 1988) adds to the general discussion of the blockade and the blockade runners.

Numerous articles have been authored by individuals in Florida and elsewhere that deal with portions of the theme of this book. David Coles, Joe Knetsch, Irvin D.S. Winsboro, George Pearce, Tracy Jean Revels, Zach Waters, Canter Brown Jr. and James P. Jones are just a few professionals who have added tremendously to the available literature of Florida in the Civil War. Many of their articles were published in the *Florida Historical Quarterly* and other historical journals in the Sunshine State. The Florida Historical Society has recently reprinted a collection of twelve articles that appeared in the *Quarterly* in a volume, *Florida's Civil War: Explorations into Conflict, Interpretations and Memory* (Florida Historical Society Press, 2007), edited by Irvin D.S. Winsboro. Most of these articles are now available online.

To follow the ebb and flow of naval actions along the coasts of Florida, the most important single source is the *Official Records of the Union and Confederate Navies in the War of the Rebellion,* a searchable compact disc that includes official orders and reports to and from ship commanders. A comparable searchable compact disc is available that contains the 128 volumes of the *Official Records of the Union and Confederate Armies in the War of the Rebellion.* These discs are offered at a nominal price by the Guild Press of Indiana and are essential research tools for any Civil War historian.

Biographical information on many of the leaders—North and South—provides additional information about how the blockade worked, its effectiveness and Confederate efforts to circumvent it.

Researching the Civil War in Florida is an exciting activity. The resources are plentiful and readily available to the diligent scholar.

About the Authors

Nick Wynne is the author or co-author of several books and has won several awards for his writing. The former executive director of the Florida Historical Society, he is also a veteran of twenty years in college classrooms. He resides with his wife, Debra, and two cats in Rockledge, Florida.

Joseph Crankshaw is an award-winning veteran Florida journalist who has written extensively on Florida history for the *Florida Times-Union*, the *Miami Herald* and Scripps Treasure Coast Newspapers. He has published articles in many other newspapers, the *National Guardsman* and Civil War history magazines; is author of "Stuart," a short history of that community; and has been a co-author or contributing writer for many publications. In 2008, the Florida Historical Society gave him the Dorothy Dodd Lifetime Achievement Award for his writings on Florida history. He holds a degree in history and political science from Stetson University. A veteran of the Korean War, he lives with his wife, Cynthia, in Stuart.